T0095538

an ADVENTURE in MISSIONS

A Practical Guide to Missions

STANLEY R FOSTER

WestBow
PRESS
A DIVISION OF THOMAS NELSON

All scripture quotations, unless otherwise indicated, are taken from the New King James Version ®. Copyright © 1982 by Thomas Nelson, Inc. Used by permission. All rights reserved.

Cover Design:
Rob Woodrum

Editor:
Bradley Woodrum

WestBow Press books may be ordered through booksellers or by contacting:

WestBow Press
A Division of Thomas Nelson
1663 Liberty Drive
Bloomington, IN 47403
www.westbowpress.com
1-(866) 928-1240

ISBN: 978-1-4497-5103-6 (hc)
ISBN: 978-1-4497-5101-2 (sc)
ISBN: 978-1-4497-5102-9 (e)
Library of Congress Control Number: 2012908782

Printed in the United States of America

WestBow Press rev. date: 07/26/2012

CONTENTS

DEDICATION

This is dedicated to those seeking direction in their life with a desire in their heart to serve the Lord. I'm passing on the things I've gained through experience and together we're building a beautiful story.

INTRODUCTION

This is a roadmap to missions and a basic resource manual. It traces the missionary experience, from the call to service and preparation, to the dazzling experience of missionary life.

This is an adventure story, but it's really His Story. It's a collection of my experiences in missions serving the Lord, and it's written for fellow believers to build on. Missions have been the grandest adventure of my life, and I hope my experiences will help others find their grandest adventure too.

This is an overview of my forty-seven year journey beginning with God's calling in 1960, through thirty years in the business world, to take the big step into ministry in 1992, and finally, taking a break in 2007. I cover the decision-making process that led me to take the big step into the world of missions by tracing the path of when the Lord called me to when I actually went into missions. Many of these experiences will provide useful guidelines for those considering missions or ministry.

My first big step was flying to Kiev, Ukraine, in January 1994. When I arrived, I had no idea what foreign missions was about or the role language and cultural adjustment would play. The Navigators ministry gave me the task of Director of Operations and Logistics in Eastern Europe. I could do the work, but I doubted whether I could adapt to living in Ukraine and Russia. This was an adventure: sometimes it was good; sometimes it was scary; sometimes I loved it; sometimes I wondered how I got into this; and sometimes I wondered how I was going to get out of it!

Trust in the Lord with all your heart, and lean not on your own understanding; in all your ways acknowledge Him, and he will direct your paths.

—Proverbs 3:5 (NKJV)

ACKNOWLEDGMENTS

Many people have invested in the person I am today. Thanks to my friend Bob Handley who invited me to church on Good Friday, 1960, to hear Dr. J. Vernon McGee. The following Sunday, I made a decision that changed my life forever. I'm eternally grateful for our friendship and your faithfulness over the years.

My Pastor and friend, Dr. Bob Zuhl, helped me transition from the business world to the ministry world. He never gave up on me. Another pastor and friend for many years is Rob Woodrum, Pastor of Eastgate Christian Fellowship. I'm very grateful for Bertha Brazie, a co-worker in the ministry and on the mission field. She has a unique talent of seeing the good in people and trying to help them.

I'm especially thankful for Jack and Shirley Whalen who prayed for me for many years while I traveled to some pretty dicey places. I always felt assured knowing Jack was covering me in prayer from his prayer closet every evening at 9:00 p.m.

I have many friends with Youth With A Mission such as Lynn Green in Harpenden, England, and Jaime Arujo in Brazil and others too numerous to mention.

My old buddy Dave Hines always had a room for me when I came to Florida. Stew L. encouraged me in missions and always held an open door to join him in ministry. I must give a huge thanks to Janice Ross, who will be a friend forever. She put up with too much from me, but because of her prayers, forgiveness, and help, I'm the person I am today.

Of course, my wife Sharon is an encourager in all I do. My brother Bob, besides being a good person, is a wordsmith. I would like to give a special thanks to my friend Bradley Woodrum for editing this manuscript and making it readable. Thank you, Bradley.

Most of all, I thank my Lord Jesus Christ, who purchased my salvation long before I was born. I echo the Apostle Paul in Galatians 2:20:

> *I have been crucified with Christ, it's not I who live but Christ lives in me; and the life which I now live in the flesh I live by faith in the Son of God, who loved me and gave his life for me.*—*Galatians 2:20 (NKJV)*

Thank you for those words, Paul.

Be a "**Hero.**" **He**ar, **R**espond, and **O**bey
(Taken from Romans 6:17 NKJV).

Stan Foster

Introduction to missions

Long before I actually entered missions, the Lord spoke clearly to me and said, "Someday you'll be a missionary." I scoffed every time I heard this! How could this ever possibly happen to me? I was far from ministry, let alone the world of missions. I had no skills for this, or so I thought, anyway.

This book is an overview to prepare for the journey and to relate some of the things a missionary can expect along the way. Hopefully there will be fewer surprises, frustrations, and casualties after reading this book. And even if you feel a little overwhelmed, this will be an encouragement. God is faithful to honor obedience. When He calls a believer to missions, He will not forget them.

I have had many incredible experiences in sixteen years of missions and ministry. I have met some people who know the Lord and are serving Him in remote places that we never hear about in the newspapers. I did not know how amazing life would be in serving the Lord. I knew very little of what I was getting into at the time I began. However, as God said to Abraham, "Go," and he went, so God said to me, "Go," and I went.

I found that when God calls someone to missions, their learned skills are not as necessary or important as their natural talents and past experiences. He will use what He has given you. Even though it may seem scary at times, God's calling will be a natural fit for you. Every calling is personal and unique, and will be "for such a time as this . . ."

The first mission venture

It was about thirty-five years between when the Lord first spoke to me about missions and when I actually entered missionary service. Many times He said, "Someday you'll be a missionary," and it was as clear as if He had spoken to me audibly. I had been a computer systems specialist for Unisys Corporation, and my career was my highest agenda. I was with the company for twenty-eight years, entering my high-earning years before retirement. During those years, my response to thoughts of missions was, "Fat chance!"

In 1991, I was promoted to a higher paying position. However, the Lord also began asking me to come to work for *Him* for no pay.

My habit was to read a chapter in the Bible in the morning and a chapter in the evening. At one point as I was studying 1 Samuel, chapters 1 and 2, but I got nothing from the reading. I read them several times and still got nothing. I decided God must have included these chapters in the Bible for some reason. But what was the reason? I then decided not to read another chapter until God revealed to me why *these* chapters were in the Bible and what they meant.

Every night, I would read the same chapters in the book of Samuel. I would get nothing as usual and close the book. I continued each evening to ask the Lord why He wrote this and what it meant. Then one night about two weeks later, I was reading the same chapters as I had been doing, but this night I began to understand them. I couldn't put them down! I read these two chapters over and over for about two weeks, and I was blessed every time I read them. God had my attention! At this point I realized in a new way that God hears and answers our prayers, and I could trust the Lord to answer my prayers.

Samuel, chapters 1 and 2, are how Samuel's mother Hannah prayed for a son and dedicated him to the Lord. Eli the priest thought she was drunk because as she was praying in silent prayer, her lips moved, but Eli heard no sound. However, God heard Hannah's silent prayer of dedication and answered her with a son who became one of the major prophets of the Old Covenant. Hannah's silent prayer went right by Eli the Priest to the throne of God. In the same way, our prayers bypass this earthly realm and go directly to the throne of God. Nothing in this earthly realm and nothing in the spiritual realm can prevent our prayers from reaching the Father in heaven.

The Lord's call on my life for missions became progressively stronger over time. I knew where God wanted me to go, but I was a little frightened to take the big step because it would be a *very* big step. He was asking me to leave my job and enter into a ministry serving Him. I did not feel prepared for this.

I began seeking the Lord for confirmation. I sought help from several local pastors, but all I got was some trite prayers and no guidance, satisfaction, or help. I thought, "I know Jesus is who He says He is, and He'll do what He says He'll do, and this decision will prove it one way or the other in my life. If this doesn't work, I'll be committing career suicide."

The following Friday evening, I prayed, "Lord, if you want me to serve you, have the company make a voluntary layoff available on the bulletin board on Monday morning!" This was a bold statement, but it would prove once and for all if I was being called to serve the Lord and to missions. It was a peaceful weekend because I had made a decision I could live with—at least for the weekend.

Well, wouldn't you know it!? Monday morning at 8:00 A.M., there was a notice on the bulletin board asking for volunteers for a layoff. I thought, "Where did this come from? Is this an answer to prayer, or what?"

The Lord answered my prayer and now it was my turn. Was I going to do what I said I would do or not? I imagined as though I was in an airplane, at an unknown altitude, blindfolded, and the Lord was asking me to step out of the plane. Whew! This was crunch time.

If I signed the layoff paperwork, there would be no more salary, no visible means of support, and no turning back. My high earning years would be cut off, and I had no outside assurance I was not making a huge mistake by doing this. The Lord simply said; "Trust me. Step out."

I decided to go for it and submitted the paperwork that morning for the voluntary layoff. After twenty-eight years with the company, I thought, "This is going to prove it once and for all," but within a few hours the euphoria wore off and I wondered if I had acted in haste.

Within a few days, I was given a two-week notice and I began to think I had gone crazy. However, it was too late to cancel the layoff process, so the decision was sealed. I was stepping out of my airplane.

I guess some might call this a step of faith, but it sure did not feel like faith; it felt risky and almost a little foolish. But God carried me through my fear and led me to a great adventure. This proves to me that Jesus is who He says He is, and He will do what He says He will do.

When I left the company, I received enough severance to get me through the first year. That was over nineteen years ago, and Jesus has not failed me even one day since then! Surely, Jesus *is* who He says He is, and He *will* do what He says He will do! That step from the airplane was faith in action. It wasn't "presumption in action," there was no presumption about it. It was faith in action—but action with fear too.

I did not presume the Lord would be there for me when He urged me to take that step. He assured me that He would be there when He said, "Trust me." There's a big difference between faith and presumption. Presumption can get you killed, but faith and His assurance will carry you through anything.

My first days in Ukraine

In the early hours of January 31, 1994, I stepped off the Lufthansa Airlines flight from Frankfort, Germany, to Kiev, Ukraine. I remembered the Lord telling me, "Someday you'll be a missionary," and here it was happening as he said. He meant what He said years before, and I was awestruck with praise.

The Soviet Union was gone in name but not in spirit, and I was an American looking at about twenty soldiers with AK-47 rifles. My first time in Ukraine was kind of a shock as the country was still freshly liberated from Communism and there were many soldiers present. I thought, "What's a nice guy like me doing in a place like this? Maybe I took one flight too many!"

Welcome to missions!

The soldiers were all business as I went down the passenger ramp to the waiting cattle van that would take us to the passenger terminal. When our luggage arrived on a hay wagon, I began to wonder how I was going to survive this experience.

This was my first mission adventure. I did not know what to expect. The culture of Ukraine was Eastern European and the predominant language was Russian. I had been interested in Russian history for a couple of years out of curiosity, but living in the former Soviet Union was very different than reading about it. I had little frame of reference and little idea of what I was getting into. I soon found that God had brought me where He wanted me for such a time as this.

As the Navigators Director of Operations for Ukraine, I was responsible for all education materials coming into the country and for the material distribution to the teams in a number of cities from the Triad organization based in Moscow,. Triad supplied all of the teaching and training materials for the Co-Mission teams throughout the former Soviet Union.

The Navigators and Campus Crusade divided the cities of the former Soviet Union so there was no overlap of resources. However, in the larger cities, such as Kiev, the need was overwhelming and both ministries worked together. The Navigators were given the task of working in the grade schools and high schools, while Campus Crusade was tasked with working in the universities.

I coordinated logistics for the Navigator teams throughout Ukraine and worked closely with the Campus Crusade Director in Kiev. The two ministries shared housing, office space, resources, and—in a sense—workers. For the Navigators, I provided medical support, arranged housing, and found meeting and office facilities for the teams when they came to Kiev. I also worked closely with Presbyterian Overseas Missions in Odessa, providing the support they needed. They did not have support available, so I filled the gap. Going into the position, I did not expect to be so busy, but I wore several hats for several organizations. The work of missions is a full time job and it can be very physically tiring.

One of my tasks in Ukraine and Russia was paying the expenses for the Navigator teams when they were away from their city and perhaps out of country. At the end of December, 1994, I had to go from Kiev to Rovno, to a town near the Caucuses Mountains, to pay rents, salaries, and utility bills for one of the Navigator teams who were in a conference out of the country. My interpreter, Boris, wanted to stop at his home village of Rokeetno to attend a wedding on the way.

The train left Kiev about six in the evening and we arrived at his village sometime after midnight. Staying there several days, we had a wonderful time with his parents and friends. I felt very privileged to meet them and be a guest in their home. They suffered greatly under the Communists but endured the abuse because of their faith, becoming humble and strong Christians. They were everything a Christian is supposed to be and more. I was amazed at what the fire of persecution can produce in a person's life, and I was humbled because I had not experienced the persecution they had endured.

When we were leaving, we could only get tickets on a train that was leaving about 1 A.M., and the only space available was in an open car with bench seats. We made it to the train and, as we picked up travelers along the way, our car filled to standing room only. During the ride, many people wanted to talk to me, probably just to listen to English spoken smoothly. They were teachers, trades people, and professional people from all walks of life. The warmth and friendliness of the Eastern European people struck me, even in their poverty. During the Cold War period, these people were forced to be at war with the west when war was not in their heart. This was another wonderful surprise. People are the same no matter where you go; their wants and needs are the same no matter what their culture.

By the time we arrived at Rovno, it was about 5:00 in the morning and there were so many people packed in our car we could not move to the door. What were we to do? We had to get off the train here and now! The passengers must have been familiar with this situation because they picked us up and passed us over their heads like logs, hand-by-hand to the door.

I went first, followed by my bag, then Boris, followed by his bag. We were passed quite gently over everyone's head to the door. I've never exited a train like this before or since. I wish I'd had a camera to record it.

As Director of Operations, I was responsible for keeping the financial security and operations functioning smoothly for teams in different cities. I was entrusted with large sums of money for paying missionary team expenses, in different cities, such as rents, utilities, transportation expenses, and emergency funds in different cities in Ukraine and Russia. I dressed as if I was a poor person, even though there were times that I carried over $38,000 on my body or had that much and more hidden in my room.

There is a good chance I would not have lived to see the next sunrise if it were publicly known I had this much money with me. When people are hungry, they do things they might not otherwise do. Even indigenous friends do things they might not otherwise do. Trust your contacts, but do not trust them with everything. Listen to your instincts, that small little voice that says "Be careful." I acted like I was living back in New York City and things were fine. I trusted to a point.

Do not reveal to anyone how much money you are hiding or carrying. When going on an outing, try to take only two or three times what is needed or can be comfortably carried. Leave the rest in a safe place—a hidden place. Emergencies will come up, so this amount should cover any contingencies.

The military police come for a "friendly" visit

In 1994, I was doing team setup for the Navigators for the Co-Mission Project in the former Soviet Union, in the city of Vinnitsa, Ukraine. I was trying to recruit interpreters, drivers, helpers, and cooks, while also finding apartments to rent for the American team due in four weeks. I also bought washing machines and dryers for each of the apartments I rented.

One day, my interpreter, Boris, wanted to go fishing, so I was on my own for the whole day. I was really looking forward to this. Surprisingly, a couple of plain clothes police officers stopped by the apartment that morning at 8:30. I guessed they just wanted to say, "Hello," and check my visa. Instead, they invited me to the police station for questioning.

Their English language skills were pretty limited. The few things they could say in English included: "You come," "You sit," and "You stay." I felt like a dog. Their car was cramped by American standards—something the size of a small compact with four doors. I knew they were military police when I got in the car because I recognized a hat in the back seat. It was an Army officer's military police hat with a red band around it. It was like the souvenir hat I had in my room back in Kiev. Little did I know there was a secret army base just outside of the city of Vinnitsa and little did I know the restaurant I liked to have lunch in once in a while was a also a favorite of many off-duty Army officers from the secret army base.

They took me in their tiny car to a regional police station of some kind. After some delay, they took me to another local police station. I was beginning to worry. The police station was more like a secure garrison with brick and concrete walls around it and broken glass on the top. The walls were about eight feet high and two feet thick. The officers took me through a big iron entrance gate, and when the gate closed, I felt like this wasn't going to be much of a day off for me.

It was an old building, typical of government buildings in the former Soviet Union. It was well-made and well-used. We went to the second floor, and we were directed by the officer at the front desk to go to a certain room down the hall. Two other officers joined us. I didn't feel good about this at all. There were four of them and one of me.

Then the questioning began.

Soviet-style military police interrogation is not something I would recommend for recreation. I was in a room with bars on the windows, about fifteen feet away from the entrance to the holding cell for prisoners. After four hours of grilling from Army Colonel Kozechenko and his three helpers, I was sweating and wondering if I would ever get out of this police station to see the sun again. Never mind ever getting back home again!

I had no phone connection back to Kiev and only crude e-mail capability. The Navigators and Campus Crusade directors knew only that I was in Vinnitsa setting up for the team coming in four weeks. No one knew I was in the police station, and no one knew what was happening in the police station. That was the worst part. The interrogation was intense and I recognized them playing "Good Cop / Bad Cop" with me. Three of them were asking me questions at the same time. It was stressful to say the least.

The interrogation lasted for hours.

What are you doing here in Vinnitsa? Why are you here? Where are you from? Where were you born? Who do you work for? Who do you work with? How much are you paid? Who pays your salary? Where do you get your money from? Who authorized you to be here in Vinnitsa? When did you arrive here? Where do you live in Kiev? How old are you? Where do you live in America? What do you do in America? What were you doing in Moscow? How long were you in Moscow? How long were you in Leningrad? What were you doing in Leningrad?

Everyone in the room got in on the questioning except for one interrogator. I guess he was the "Good Cop." He did seem like a nice guy too. As I look back, I think perhaps they just wanted to hear English spoken smoothly without a Russian or Ukrainian accent, but they were intense about it. Through all this, I tried to maintain the persona of a person who was not very important in the scheme of things. I could not answer a lot of their questions because I did not know. Actually, I knew a lot, but it would have compromised the Navigators and Campus Crusade operation in Kiev if I told them all they wanted. So I played dumb. After all, I was just a guy trying to help out where I could.

During the interrogation, I focused more on the humanitarian aspect of our mission in Ukraine and Russia. People were receiving Christ as their savior, and I did not want to endanger that activity. New believers were coming under the interrogation process too. A very dear friend in Vinnitsa was interrogated by the same KGB officers after it was discovered he had become a believer. He had been a Communist all of his life until he saw *The Jesus Film* and put his faith in Christ. He and I would walk in a park for hours where he asked me many questions about his newfound faith. There are no microphones in public parks, so they were a safe place to talk. We could talk freely and I was able to answer his questions without worrying about the listening ears of the police.

After my interrogation, I had to go to the regional government's administration office to get a letter authorizing me to be in this city and in this region. I had to get the invitation letter authorizing me to be in Vinnitsa from his office, signed by him, and then return to the police station the next day. If I couldn't get the letter and authorization, I had two days to be out of Ukraine or I would be arrested and sent to jail.

In spite of my situation, I had a secret weapon: My prayer partner, Jack Whalen. Jack prayed for me every evening, he and his wife Shirley have been a gift to me from the Lord "for such a time as this." I've been in similar circumstances, but I always knew Jack was praying for me. It was such a comfort to know God is faithful to watch over us and answer our prayers.

It is wise to have prayer partners who will faithfully support you in prayer even though you are not in daily contact. The local telephone service was poor at best in the rural towns like this. There was no way they could know I was in trouble unless the Lord told them.

Always have a faithful prayer partner on your side who will keep you in prayer for a covering of the blood of Jesus and a hedge of protection around you. I knew Jack and Shirley were not aware of my situation, but I knew they would be praying for me. It seemed like the Lord reminded me He had people praying for me. I remembered this while I was being interrogated and that was a great comfort even though I seemed to be in serious trouble.

What you see is what you eat and other things I learned

When I went to the Regional Director's office for my authorization letter allowing me to be in Vinnitsa, the director was at his dacha in the country for the summer. That was a potential problem for me. A *dacha* is a family farm in the country with no phone communication of any kind. However, *by coincidence*, he was expected to return to his office that afternoon for some administrative function. Talk about coincidences! Isn't God the God of circumstances? God brought him back in his office that afternoon just to sign the invitation and authorization letter I needed—that day! There really are no coincidences in God's economy.

The regional government office building was as new and modern as anything in the western world. I located his secretary quite easily and she spoke very smooth English. She had a well-made and well-used desk and her office was bright and clean. While I was waiting for the administrator to arrive, she asked me to share lunch with her. Of course I had to accept her offer because it would have been a cultural slap in the face if I said, "No." Well, she pulled an old cooked cow's tongue from her desk. It was perhaps wrapped in something like a sheet of newspaper; I'm not sure, but it didn't look good. I could not make it look like a McDonald's cheeseburger no matter how hard I tried.

My thoughts were: "Oh God! I need your help NOW!" If I refused her gesture of friendship, it would have been a deep insult to her. And I needed her friendship in order for the paperwork to go smoothly.

I remembered a previous train trip from Leningrad to Moscow where I wanted to brush my teeth in the lavatory. I wondered how potable the water was since I could see the ground through the holes in the floor. I prayed for God's protection and brushed my teeth. Other missionaries I knew contracted serious stomach illnesses from drinking public water in Russia. I remembered His protection then on the train and asked the secretary if I could pray for God's blessing over our shared meal. After prayer, I proceeded to chew on this thing she sliced off for me. It tasted like meat, but I shudder when I think about it. It could have been a disaster, but God protected me from harm and I made friends with the secretary. The director arrived about an hour later and signed my invitation and authorization letter. This was a major milestone for me because I had the letter in my hand and I met a very nice person that day.

The next day, my interpreter, Boris, showed up at my apartment from his fishing trip. I told him what had happened. We went to the police station with the invitation and authorization from the Regional Director to report to the police officers. He recognized the "police officers" when he saw them; they were KGB agents. These same agents of the KGB, the Komitet Gosudarstvennoi Bezopasnosti or the Committee for State Security, had been at Boris's parent's home a few years prior looking for Bibles. The Bibles were stored under his bed, but when the agents moved his bed to look under it, the Bibles stayed under the bed as it slid along. When the officers didn't see the Bibles, they moved the bed back and, of course, the Bibles slid back with the bed. Isn't it amazing how God works? I'm probably the only Navigator staff member to be interrogated by the KGB.

It's not uncommon for situations like this happen with frequency on the mission field. The lesson here is to pray hard when you are not sure of the quality of food or drink set before you. There are different cultural factors involved with most every meal; do your best to remember this and God will take care of the results. It would be safe to say as a guideline to pray and trust and pray, then do what you have to do.

Angels unawares

One evening in Vinnitsa, I was really tired. I had been looking for apartments all day, and at about 8 P.M., I decided to walk back to the hotel instead of taking the tram. I wanted to enjoy the evening air and some peace. I was walking along Lenin Street and I had to cross the Ushneboog River to the hotel.

Along the way, there were some ruffians on my side of the street, and I thought it would be better to cross the street and avoid them, rather risk a confrontation. I had just had my session with the police and was not in the mood for a similar adventure. However, I thought, "God has sent me here, and I'm here under His authority."

I then decided that I was not going to cross the street to avoid these punks and if we tangle up in a confrontation, so be it. I kept walking straight and with a little more vigor too. These ruffians were harassing the *babushkas* (older ladies) by knocking over their grocery wagons and being generally nasty little kids. I had run into kids like this in Leningrad, so I was prepared for something to happen. I had determined not to back down but to claim this street for Christ. I kept walking, expecting trouble.

Without hearing a sound, a huge Russian soldier in uniform, about 6'6", came bounding in a full run toward those ruffians. He passed me on my left, less than a foot from me. I did not hear him until he was directly at my side and going by me. It should have been very easy to hear him even walking; he was wearing those heavy Russian military "Jack" boots that made a clomping sound when they walked. He headed for those ruffian kids and when I got to the corner, they were gone and so was he. I thought, "This is my street. Praise God! It may be called Lenin Street but this is God's street and He gave it to me."

I truly believe God sent an angel to clear the way for me when I decided to act in faith and God's authority in that situation. Things like this are not uncommon in missions, but in my experiences, when it was all over, the "angel" disappears quickly. Is our God awesome or what?

Listening to that still small voice

It seems like I've grown in Christ with every single mistake or bad choice I've made. Every bad decision had some kind of pain attached to it and a lesson to be learned. One lesson I have learned from making bad choices is to listen to the Lord. I mean to actively listen for His voice.

One important learning experience started in September, 1996. I attended the Discipleship Training School (DTS) with Youth With A Mission (YWAM) at the Rose River Retreat Center in Virginia. I completed the DTS program in December and started working in the accounting office in Richmond.

I had worked about a month in the accounting office and some friends asked me to go skiing with them in the mountains of Virginia. These were not like the mountains I was used to in Colorado, but—nevertheless—a day on the ski slopes is better than a day at work. His voice may be a still, small, quiet whisper, but on January 27, 1997, I wish He would have shouted in my ear something like, "Don't go skiing today, Stanley, or you'll regret it. This is Jesus talking to you. Listen to me." I think I'm still learning to hear His voice today.

I was a good skier; I have two silver medals and a gold medal from NASTAR competitive downhill skiing at Keystone Colorado in 1991. However, when the staff of YWAM Virginia planned a ski trip to the mountains (hills) of Virginia and asked me to go with them, the Lord told me not to go in strong emotional feelings. He warned me a number of times and gave me bad feelings about the trip up to the time my friends came to pick me up.

When they came to the door on January 28 at 5:30 in the morning, with the promise of a good cup of coffee and great camaraderie, I decided to go anyway. When we were in the car, driving to the mountains, the Lord stopped telling me not to go. He did not tell me anything more. I guess He gave up because I refused to listen. We had a nice trip to the mountains, but I didn't hear anything more from the Lord.

Just before noon, everyone wanted to make one more run before we broke for lunch. I didn't want to make another run because I was tired and just wanted to head to the lodge for lunch. It was a Black Diamond run, the most difficult type of run, which was no problem for me, but, again, I let myself be talked into doing something I didn't feel good about because I was with good friends. Bob Ruthazer and John Henry were there, and were both good friends and longtime YWAMers from Virginia.

As I was coming down the run, I encountered a large rise where I would have to "take air" to go over it. I decided to slalom to the left and bypass the air opportunity. As I did so, the embankment gave away and I went face first into a rock and then flipped upside down into a tree. Bob was the first one to get to me and he got me down from the tree. It took the Ski Patrol thirty minutes to get me back up to the ski path and then down to the waiting ambulance for the ride to the hospital. I was unconscious and if it was not for Bob, I may not have made it because I was losing fluid from my nose. It seems like the Lord had Bob there at the right time to help me.

The hospital emergency room staff at the first hospital told my friends that I would not live until midnight. I had several severe brain hemorrhages, and they were not equipped to deal with such injuries. They decided the only chance I had to live was to get me to Virginia's main trauma center in Charlottesville, about seventy miles away. The doctors decided I could not survive the trip by ambulance, so they took me by helicopter.

When we arrived in Charlottesville, the Intensive Care Unit doctors decided I had too much brain damage and they couldn't help me. They also said I would not live past midnight. The guys I had been skiing with had driven to the first and the second hospital. They called the YWAM base in Richmond with the news. The base shut down for four days of on-going, around the clock intercessory prayer. They e-mailed prayer requests throughout the world in a worldwide YWAM prayer network. I woke up two days later in a pretty incoherent state, but alive to the surprise of the doctors and nurses.

The first two people that came to see me were Stew Lieberman and Bob Ruthazer. Stew was my YWAM Discipleship Training School leader from Rose River, Virginia, and Bob was a faithful friend. These two are rough-looking characters, and when I saw them in my incoherent state, I thought they were hit-men from New York. I don't know where this thought came from, but I asked who they were and they introduced themselves. I still did not recognize the names even though I had known them very well before the accident. I pretended to know who they were even though I still did not really remember them. My memory was shot.

A week or so later, I was put in therapy to relearn how to walk and talk. My brain was pretty scrambled. A few days later the nurses in front of me appeared to only have a half of a face. In fact, all the nurses in the room had only half of a face. One half was completely blank. I told this to the nurse who was standing next to me and they took me for another C.A.T. Scan immediately. My brain was hemorrhaging again. They immediately took me to the Department of Neurosurgery at Virginia Commonwealth University (VCU) for surgery the next morning.

After surgery to block off the new hemorrhages and remove several existing blood clots, I began a period of recovery. It took a full year to recover physically and my mental recovery has been an ongoing process. I have had to learn to spell many words again and my grammar is damaged to this day. However, I am relearning all the time and spell-check is wonderful.

It seems most of the problems I have experienced resulted from not listening to His still, small, and quiet voice amidst the clamor of other voices. The enemy—or even friends—can make the clamor so loud it is hard to hear His voice, and it is not until it was all over that I remembered hearing His voice. When my prayer life diminishes or when my Bible study diminishes, I seem to have difficulty hearing His voice. These are two vital factors in hearing the voice of the Lord.

Sometimes the Lord speaks through circumstances. He also speaks through the Word of God, or by a "Word" spoken through a Godly friend, or sometimes it is a simple pull on the heart that will lead to the right direction. He has also been known to speak in an audible voice and you'll know His voice when your hear it! There will be no question when He speaks.

I recovered from the ski accident in January and the neural surgery in February to function again in the accounting office by May. I was able to begin my class outreach in June. I went with another YWAM team going on outreach to work on a Kibbutz in Northern Galilee, Israel. We were there for ten weeks, and I continued to recover almost on a daily basis.

God is the Master of our decisions

After we returned home from outreach in August, another YWAM school seemed interesting to me. This was the School of Jewish Studies (SJS), scheduled for September on the YWAM base in Richmond, Virginia. I thought it might be nice to know something Jewish since the Bible had a lot to do with the Jewish people, after all. Who knows? If I ever taught a Sunday school class, I might need to know something like this. I was not particularly drawn to this school, but I eased into it from a point of curiosity and uncertainty.

There were no other choices competing for my attention at the time, so why not take the course? Since I didn't have a reason *not* to take it, I signed up. Oddly, I made the *right* decision for a very *weak* reason.

Attending this school was exactly where the Lord wanted me. The YWAM School of Jewish Studies brought a major shift in my theology and anchored my faith in Christ like no other course I had taken up to this point in my life. I was energized to the

Jewishness of scripture and how I, as a Gentile, was included in God's plan from the ages past to the ages future. I felt rejuvenated with new life and a commitment that was revolutionary. Around that time, I also attended the Tikvat Israel Messianic Jewish Congregation in Richmond.

When I finished the YWAM School of Jewish Studies, I went on another outreach to Kibbutz Dafna in Israel. When I returned a few months later, I was asked to be the bookkeeper for YWAM Virginia. Being the base bookkeeper was not what I had planned to do, but I did not have anything else on my agenda. I had some courses in accounting at the University of Maryland and my training with Unisys Corporation allowed me to make an easy transition into bookkeeping and office administration. Sometimes it seems like we just fall into God's plan for our life without even sensing it. Then, only later, do we realize we are in the right place—and we were prepared for it.

After taking the School of Jewish Studies, my theology and ministry took on a Messianic focus. The Bible is God's Word: the Old Covenant and New Covenant were written by God's chosen people, the Jews, as the Holy Spirit guided them. Jewish believers today seem to have a revelatory understanding of scripture that Gentiles generally do not seem to have. In general, we tend to read scripture for its surface value and the meanings from the Greek and Hebrew languages, but Jewish believers seem to have a deeper sense of understanding of scripture. God loves the Jewish people as much as He does Gentiles, but he has a covenant with the Jewish people from the time of Abraham that is still in effect today. I have found the understanding of the culture and traditions of the Jewish people will bring scripture to a deeper level of understanding.

The subtleties and depth of scripture seem hidden to the Gentile mind. Even though we are grafted in, we have to be rewired to understand. The Jewish mindset, the language, and customs of the Jewish people are all woven into scripture. It takes a Jewish believer, already steeped in God's story, who understands the language and customs of the Jewish people, to unravel the deepest meanings of scripture and bring them to light.

I remember how rich the Wednesday evening Torah Studies were at Tikvat Israel Messianic Jewish Congregation. Rabbi Jamie Cowen led this study, and it was the richest Bible study I ever attended. He could unfold storylines from scripture that were hidden and could not be seen without binoculars of understanding—the Hebrew language, along with the customs and traditions of the people.

After attending Tikvat Israel Messianic Jewish Congregation for a few years, I realized I am not Jewish and I never will be Jewish. I'm a Gentile and I'm perfectly happy being a Gentile. After all these years, I have adjusted to it; it's become like an old shoe to me. I have no desire to be Jewish, but I love the Jewish people and support them in their Jewishness. I'm a happy Gentile camper. I love the Jewish people as God loves the Jewish people. After all, Jesus is a Jew. Moreover, I believe I'd love the Jewish people even if God didn't love them.

My seemingly casual decision to take the YWAM School of Jewish Studies brought about a major shift in my doctrinal understanding. All of this was in God's plan for my life and it turned out to be a major blessing. God was indeed in subtle control of my decisions, even though I made the decision to attend this school, God had a blessing waiting there for me. I learned God is the master of our decisions. Faith and trust, and seeking God's best allowed the Lord to move me in the right place at the right time.

God is our master and the master of our circumstances. We are His children; He cares for us and will not lead us into temptation, and the circumstances that come into our life are not for our hurt but for our good. Situations in the beginning that appear to be for our hurt will turn out for our good in the end. We will grow stronger as we are being conformed into the image our His beloved son, our Lord Jesus.

The Lord remembers what you say even if you forget!

Sometimes there are not many assurances in making the right decision, but then the circumstances line up and the Lord confirms the decision in the results. For several years I told the Lord, "I'll go wherever You want me to go, but *not* to China! I'd rather go to the moon! No good thing ever came out of China! And is Chinese even a real language?" Telling the Lord something like this is a good way to get to China. This was really immature and silly of me.

In the summer of 1999, I was asked to go to Beijing, China, for thirty days as part of a creative access mission conference. I was the bookkeeper and banker, and I also taught one segment in the conference. I decided to take about twenty packets of Starbucks coffee with me thinking, "These poor people have never had a good cup of coffee in their entire lives." What an attitude I had! I was filled with preconceived ideas, unfounded opinions, and arrogance.

The day we left, our flight was late leaving, so we missed our connecting flight to Beijing. The team worried that this was going to cause us a serious problem, but I was the oddball: I felt an excitement that God was going to do something special. As it turned out, since we missed our flight, the airline provided a nice hotel room in San Francisco, dinner, breakfast, and all local transportation. Then they put us in the first-class section on the next flight to Beijing. We had a beautiful dinner, a wonderful night's rest, and it turned out to be a wonderful twelve hour flight in first class all the way.

When we landed, I had no jet lag and hit the ground running. Driving to our destination in the city, I was surprised to see McDonalds, Burger King, Kentucky Fried Chicken, and—would you guess it—a Starbucks coffee shop one block from our hotel!

I found the people were so kindhearted and gracious. They were so curious about these "Big Nose" westerners that they would even watch us eat in restaurants. In thirty days, I had learned thirty-two things I could say in Mandarin Chinese, and they could understand me! I loved it and I loved the people! I still love the Chinese people.

The Chinese language has a number of intonations, and if a word is spoken with the wrong intonation the meaning changes. For example, if you wanted to say "Hello" and you use an incorrect intonation, you might end up ordering a swimming pool. As you can imagine, I bought a number of swimming pools. The Chinese people had many laughs at my attempts to speak their language and were so gracious to laugh with me and not at me.

I used to think a kamikaze pilot was a Japanese suicide pilot in World War II. I believe that is not correct. It is actually the Chinese rickshaw drivers I rode with. They were the kamikaze rickshaw drivers. These people do not fear buses, trucks, cars, and motorcycles and the ride is a real prayer event. One time the rickshaw's drive chain broke in the middle of the intersection of two major highways. No problem! The driver simply got off the bike and repaired the chain right there. There were buses, trucks, cars, and motorcycles going by us and around us in all directions for about twenty minutes. When he finished repairing the chain, we took off again. I had a great front seat view of Beijing traffic for about twenty minutes.

As a result of that trip to China, I fell in love with the Chinese people. My heart now yearns for the Chinese people to this day. God showed me His heart of love for them through my experiences there. He loves them as much as He loves you and me. It was silly of me to tell the Lord what I would or would not do. I spoke out of ignorance, and in His kindness, He showed me, in a loving way, there is a lot I do not know.

I'd love to go back to China, but that door is closed for me now. I accept that; knowing God's plan for my life is better than I can know or imagine. If it includes China, that would be wonderful, and if it does not, that is wonderful too. I have great respect for their language and now I'd much rather go to China than the moon.

What are your misconceptions of the field you are called to? Have you researched the field? Can you do more? The research you do before you go will pay huge dividends later. What can you do to break down the wall of misconceptions, to minimize the surprises when you "hit the ground"? The learning curve can be difficult and painful if you reach your destination with a misconceived understanding of the culture, the people, and the consequences of misunderstanding. Remember the law of unintended consequences: What you don't plan for *will* happen!

With faith, trust, and seeking God's best, He will lead you to the place He has for you, but if you get off to a wrong start or going in a wrong direction, getting you back on track can be an adventure!

Don't quit; wait on the Lord

Do not let your feelings and desires get ahead of the Lord. He uses feelings and desires to make us ready when our door opens, but do not move without His confirmation even if you are ready to move. Let Him move you but be ready.

In 2000 and 2001, I was living in England. It became quite a discouraging and stressful situation, and I couldn't see any way out of it. Even when the going got tough, I should have waited and let the Lord work on the situation; instead, I responded to the situation based on my emotions. I should have sought the Lord to let Him take action, allowing Him to show me the way from *within* the circumstances.

I brought 10 or 12 important and exciting books with me when I moved to the ministry base in England. They covered a ministry focus that did not parallel their ministry; however, they certainly would have augmented the ministry there. The ministry focus and those missionaries housed on the base would have benefited greatly from the contents of these books. The book store manager would not order them in the store. I felt he did not understand the importance of the material, but he was a store manager and that ended it.

At that same time, the mission compound received weekly food allotments from a major supermarket chain kind enough to donate food to the base. One stipulation was that we could not keep food past its expiration date. After that date it had to be destroyed. We each had a small designated section of a freezer for personal food storing. A base person was assigned to randomly inspect our food every week for expired foods, to comply with the expired date condition. One day, after removing all my food from my personal storage area, the inspector person found one small item at the bottom of the freezer with an expired product date. I was not aware this expired food was in the freezer. As a result I was denied food from the donated foods for two months. This made me mad. There was no forgiveness or accommodation for an unintentional oversight. I decided to leave at that time and made plans to move back to the United States. I didn't give the Lord a chance to work out the situation. I didn't wait for the Lord. My anger overtook me, and I left.

It turned out okay for me, but perhaps it would have turned out even better if I would have exercised some patience. Who knows where patience may have taken me? There were several people who might have made a difference in my life and several schools that might have altered the focus of my missionary service. I must trust the Lord, who is the master of circumstances, to turn my flawed decisions into good results.

The lesson here is: do not cut and run. Check with your prayer partners and listen to someone who is not in the emotion of the moment. The stress of the moment can cloud your thinking and your decision making with consequences you will have to live with. Your prayer partners are not clouded by the emotions of the moment and can see more clearly.

Decisions made in the flesh lead to wrong outcomes

We should never tell the Lord what we will or will not do. He has our best interest in mind, and while it may not seem like the right thing to do at the time, we need to trust His management of our life. Go when He says and wherever He says. Trust Him to lead, but just make sure the Holy Spirit is there. It is simple, but it can be hard to work out in real life.

I felt it was time to leave England, but I did not quite know where to go or what to do. I had lived in Florida for several years and had many friends there. So I decided to leave YWAM and move back to Florida. I got a job working at a bank. I really tried hard to do a good job and pretended to enjoy the environment, but I just didn't have a heart for being a bank teller. Consequently, I resigned.

About a month later, I took my car in for service and while chatting with the dealer's service manager, he offered me a job as a service greeter at an auto dealership. That sounded pretty good; I had never done this before and thought it might be the right thing to do. To my surprise, it was a very competitive environment. Employees slandered or blamed one another and tried to bring harm to each other's careers. Perhaps their thinking was that if the other person got fired, they would get a promotion. What an awful work environment!

It was almost a sport to hurt good people needlessly. For example, a salesman would jump in and chat briefly with another salesman's customer and then record that as having "talked" to the customer. This meant he was entitled to split the commission with the legitimate salesman. I was let go just days before my three month probationary period ended. If I had stayed three more days, I would have become a full-time employee with health benefits. Such is life in an auto dealership. Here I was unemployed and with no direction in my life.

Who knows where I would have been had I waited for God to lead me?

Enthusiasm outruns wise counsel

Shortly after that, I found a mission agency looking for people to go to China. They had an opening for a bookkeeper and office manager to work at a university north of Beijing. I applied and was accepted. My prayer partner, Jack Whalen, told me I should not go. I didn't want to hear that. I was thrilled to be able to go back to China.

My first assignment was to spend a month in Colorado learning their accounting system. To my surprise, I found the ministry in Colorado and university accounting system in Beijing was done on a spreadsheet. Chinese bank records were in shambles. Records were handwritten, faulty, or even non-existent. Some of the prior record keepers at the university were from the United States, but it was obvious that recordkeeping was not their strong point.

I spent a month auditing their ministry records for the last fiscal year. Then I spent another month or two auditing their ministry expense accounts for the last calendar year. There always seemed to be something else that had to be cleaned up that delayed my departure for Beijing.

The SARS epidemic broke out in China, and then the CEO of our ministry was diagnosed with two inoperable brain tumors. He died two months later and the income for the ministry fell into serious financial difficulty. It took $11,000 a month to run the ministry and the income fell to $2,500. The ministry was in serious trouble. About a week later, I received a bill from the federal government for $7,500 in property taxes due from the purchase of my townhouse in Florida.

I should have listened to Jack. My feelings and personal desire to return to China got ahead of God's plan for me. He closed the door to return there in order to protect me while I was still en-route. It would have been far worse and more costly to return home from China than from Evergreen, Colorado. In addition, there were more problems before I left Colorado.

The previous year, I had rolled my IRA retirement into the purchase of a house and now the Federal government wanted their taxes from my IRA immediately. I felt the Lord was not blessing this effort to go back to China.

I decided to return to Florida, get a job, and pay off my bills. By the time I left Colorado, another $2,000 was added to the debt for car repairs and other bills. So I was in debt for $9,500.

All this was within a one-week period! I think I got the message. However, there was more to come.

When I got back to Florida, my renters wanted out of my house and released from the contract. I was happy with that because I needed a place to live. After I moved back into the house, though, I found that, in the six months they rented the townhouse, they had trashed it.

The utilities were cut off for non-payment and there were fist-sized holes in the walls. I had to have it repaired and completely repainted on the inside. The carpet on the ground floor was soiled so badly that I had to have it replaced with tile. The front door was damaged and had to be replaced, including the framing, along with the front and rear screen doors. Even the barbecue grill was burned out. As a result, I decided I would never rent my house again.

Through this, I learned to not presume all feelings are from the Lord. Wait for God to move in your situation before you move. The Lord is the Lord of circumstances. Wait to see where He's working in the circumstances before moving. *Then* wait for Him to provide the energy to move. I had presumed feelings when I left England, and I had presumed feelings when I tried to go back to China. Do not make decisions based on feelings and presumptions. Wait for the Lord to confirm His leading and to move in your life circumstances before you do anything.

Heed your prayer partners

Seek wise counsel and then wait for confirmation and listen to your prayer partners, even if their counsel seems wrong. The Lord has provided them for you, and they are accountable to the Lord for the counsel they provide to you. Trust your prayer partners and your support team. They have your best interests at heart, and they are not easily swayed by the emotions of the moment. Going back to China felt right to me, but my prayer partner, Jack Whalen, told me the Lord said I should not go. I trusted my own feeling more than my trusted and faithful prayer partner. This was a big mistake on my part, and it was costly for me, in time and money.

I am a slow learner sometimes, and unfortunately, I seem to learn by experience. Listen to your prayer partners. Listen even when you do not agree with them or when you think you are more right than they are. Your prayer partners are God's gift to you and they are part of your team. They often see from afar, and you may be too deep in the woods to see the trees!

I went back to work at the bank again and paid off my debt. I knew I was called to missions and now I felt trapped in the bank. So I quit again. This time I knew I would never go back to secular work (or so I thought). The work in the bank situation had become like the auto dealership, and I just did not have a heart for it anymore.

I knew I was called to missions but just could not seem to get going. I finally decided to sell my house and just go somewhere, anywhere. My old friend Stew L, from my days with YWAM, was ministering in Israel and invited me to join him.

My house was on the market for several months and there did not seem to be any interest in it. I considered taking it off the market and going back to work again. At this point, I had pretty much used all my financial resources. So I decided to take the house off the market the following Monday and apply for a job somewhere.

On Friday afternoon, the real estate agent called to tell me he had a couple that was interested in the house and wanted to look at it Saturday morning. He asked me to be out of the house for a few hours. That seemed fine to me. I went out for a leisurely breakfast on the beach. While I waited, I told God that if the house did not sell, I would take it as a sign to stay where I am, and that I was not meant to go back to Israel.

When I got back after lunch there was a message on the answering machine; the people loved the house and made a full price offer. I immediately called back to accept the offer, and I began making plans to go to Israel the minute I got off the phone. The Lord had not forgotten me, and He still had a plan for my life! I was down to the wire on this one! So what is to be learned from this? You cannot rely on feelings and circumstances alone. Listen to your prayer partners and wait for God to open the door.

Things I've learned

Every mission field is different because the culture, values, and language are different. Still, there are basic suggested guidelines to live by. They include:

1) Stay in God's Word; do not neglect your Bible study for ministry activity
2) Keep in an attitude of prayer
3) Be alert to the leading of the Holy Spirit
4) Do not slack off in your quiet time or prayer time just because you get too busy doing the work of the ministry

You will have to spend more time with the Lord in prayer when you are overseas. The enemy may try to set a trap for you, but be on guard, even in friendly settings. There can be no compromise; one slip and there can be trouble, and this may affect the ministry. Keep your prayer partners and your support team apprised of your circumstances. I recommend a weekly update to your support team.

Some people are specifically called to be support partners. Their MOS or Military Occupational Specialty so to speak, is Prayer Partner. We are all in the same army. Where would the foot soldier be without a service and support team behind him? Support partners are the most valued assets in a soldier's arsenal when on the spiritual battlefield.

Heed your prayer partners and your support team. They are the navigators in your journey with the Lord. Trust them even if you do not always agree with them and it will save you much pain and heartache down the road. They have your best interest at heart, and they are not blinded by the emotion of the moment or the present situation you may be in.

Identification to carry in a foreign country

When you go on outreach in a foreign country, take the original documents you will need to get in and out of countries and airports. However, once you establish your base in a country, leave original copies together such as passport and accompanying documentation, visa, credit cards, driver's license, social security card, medical cards, insurance cards, membership cards, airline tickets, and other original items in a secure and safe place. Never carry original documents in your wallet or purse while you're in—country. Leave these items at home or wherever you call home at the time. Take only photocopies with you.

If your wallet or purse is lost or stolen, all you will have to replace is the money—the original documents will not be lost. They can be easily duplicated again. Being without money *and* documentation in another land is not a friendly experience for a foreigner. I had my wallet stolen in Israel, of all places, by a taxi driver. Do not count on the American Embassy to be a big friend when it is needed either. The American Embassy is there to help, but they really do not care very much. The Embassy will help with minor things but if you need to replace lost identification, money, credit cards or other assistance, they are very reluctant to be of assistance. My wallet with primary identification, credit cards and money were stolen. The embassy provided no assistance other than to record my name and address. They were not much help. Fortunately, the congregation I was working with gave me the assistance I needed to restore the credit cards and identification. But I lost $500 in cash I was going to use to repair my computer. That was a hard lesson of learning to be careful and never letting my guard down.

Sharing your wealth

As an American, you are a logical target because of the perception that all Americans are rich. There will always be those who want to take advantage of your relative or perceived wealth and would not feel bad about it. To them, this may not be stealing but more like "wealth sharing" with a feeling that they deserve to share your money.

Always reconcile your cash balance in private, even if you need to go to the restroom and lock the door to do it. Never reconcile your cash in front of other people, even if they are your team members. Indigenous people in ministry are still susceptible to wealth sharing when the opportunity presents itself. Do not think this doesn't happen! A word to the wise: Be on guard.

There are certain things you do not share, and your wallet is one of them. I advise having two wallets, one for the original documents and extra money left in a safe place and one to carry with you, your street wallet. The safe place wallet is only carried to and from permanent places of residence, like when leaving home to go to the mission field or back again. Keep it hidden and secure. Use the street wallet with copies of identification documents, and cash only; no credit cards or original driver's licenses, unless *absolutely* necessary.

In the street, only carry in your wallet the things you can afford to lose. Carry this wallet in your front pocket, not the rear pocket. A wallet in the rear pocket can be an open invitation to a pickpocket. A good moneybag is one that attaches to your belt and rides *inside* the pants. These can be purchased in stores that carry travel items or at an airport before you leave. Be sure to color the loops the same color as the belt to conceal the loops. Use a permanent felt marker to color the loops if necessary.

A woman can conceal a money belt in several other locations besides a belt, but be careful if a bulge shows. One may not be able to see the money belt, but the outline could be revealing. Loop the money pouch to your belt on the buckle side of the belt for a more secure attachment.

I've hidden money under rugs; inside, behind, and under toilet tanks; behind radiators and refrigerators; inside flowerpots; and any other place I thought no one would think to look. Another thought; there was a time when I had to refuse to allow an indigenous person to stay overnight in my apartment because of the amount of cash I had with me. He was a friend of the team, but not a member of the team. I hated to be like that, but I was responsible for a lot of money and that responsibility came above our friendship.

Keeping Receipts

Get receipts whenever possible. If something is accidentally left or dropped in the taxi when leaving, the identity of the driver or taxi will be recorded on the receipt, so there will be a good possibility of getting the items back.

In many countries, a taxi driver will give a receipt, but you may have to request it too. If the driver does not give a receipt, try to get the driver's business card for callback business when needed. He will usually welcome the opportunity for repeat business, and it is good way to get his identification too. Who knows? A relationship may develop from it also, but the important point is to have his identification for reference.

If it's not possible to get a receipt or the driver's card, write down the taxi's phone number, driver's name, date and time, and even the vehicle license number or the trip charge. Identifying information like this may be needed in the future.

Another very important thing to be aware of is to only take registered and licensed taxis. I have heard of a horrible event that happened when some missionaries arrived in a Central American country where they were picked up at the airport by a taxi driver. The driver told them, "I've come to meet you and take you to your hotel." The driver took the travelers out of the city, where he managed to rob and murder one of them. This was reported to me by an indigenous Christian from this country.

Travelers coming into a country usually carry a lot of money with them and that generates attraction. This is a true danger. The travelers in Central America were even aware of this trick, and one actually had to dive out of the moving vehicle to get away! It's okay to be trusting, but do not be unwise when you're in a situation like this. There are nasty people out there who make a living from people who trust too much.

Think smart, be safe, protect your money, protect your identification and get receipts for everything. It may seem redundant when you are collecting receipts but when you need them, redundancy is a small price to pay for the security of knowing you have the information you need to overcome a problem.

In-country dress code

Never travel alone in a country unless you speak the language fluently or there is no other choice. Always dress down; don't flaunt anything. Do not draw attention to yourself. Hide yourself in the crowd. Do not dress to say, "I'm wealthy and I have money." Do not dress like you would in your home country, but dress in clothes an ordinary indigenous person would wear.

To start with, your dress code will mark you as a foreigner, so it will be hard to blend in, but do the absolute best possible. It may require buying a new set of clothing in the country, but do it to hide your identity as a "foreigner with money." Dress like the people to which you are called to minister. Get a trusted native to help you dress right.

When I was living in Kiev, Ukraine, shortly after the Soviet Union collapsed, I attended a May Day parade. This was a large Communist parade through the center of Kiev in front of the downtown government building. There were banners and flags the length of the parade, it was quite colorful. I noticed several government police agents watching me, and I wondered why they were looking at me. They were looking at my hat and then my shoes. The shoes were from the States and not traditional

STANLEY R FOSTER

soviet peasant boots. I must have appeared as some kind of government agent. I was not aware of it, but I was also wearing a blue-grey fur hat worn by the Army security services. My dress at this Soviet parade brought unwanted attention to me. That mistake could have led to serious problems because I was not aware that what I was wearing marked me as an outsider, someone who did not belong there. My hat and shoes were simply to keep me warm, but their material and shape were out of character for the situation. The police agents did not know who or what I was, but thankfully they decided to leave me alone at the time.

Staying safe on the go

In a foreign country, we are not always alert to the ways of local people and what their activities mean. Do not allow yourself to get in a situation that might make you vulnerable; be on guard. You may be among friends, but it is better to err on the side of caution.

You can expect to be followed by government agents or by those looking to take advantage of your ignorance of their culture, the language, or just the fact that you are a foreigner. Remember, a foreign traveler is vulnerable and has very few legal resources. The indigenous member of the team may be a "plant" too. Both scenarios have happened to me, so I speak from experience. It's their country, not yours. Don't count on the American Embassy to help either; sometimes they can be more of a problem than the local government.

If there is a need to transport large amounts of cash, take only very trusted companions, those who are fluent in the language and customs of the country. Be very clandestine if there is a possibility of exposure to danger and always stay where people are. Never be lured into a dark area or away from a public place. The chances of being assaulted in a secluded area are greater than in a public place. Always be on guard, but look like you are in control and everything is okay. Be calm.

In dangerous situations, I always pretend that I am back in New York City where I grew up. I immediately go into a defensive posture. I begin looking for anyone who may be looking at me. I avoid that person, and if I am moving, I try to ditch them quickly. Trackers do not normally work alone so if you notice someone watching you, they probably have a partner in the area somewhere. Keep your personal radar antenna up.

When going somewhere, move purposefully—do not linger like you are on holiday or vacation. Act like someone is expecting you at a certain time, and they are just around the corner. Act like you know what you are doing and you know where you are going—you will appear less vulnerable. Move with purpose. Camouflage is 50% of defense in a foreign country.

Another tip is to check your watch frequently as if you are expecting to meet someone, stay in public view and keep around people. If you are being watched, try to get lost in the crowd until safe again. Perhaps you can move to another location and return if there is a need, but get off their radar screen.

Personal computer care and backup

I recommend a laptop or handheld computer that weighs less than six pounds. Do not get a desktop replacement; they weigh about eight pounds. That does not seem like much, but dragging it through airports and bus stations will cause it to feel like twenty-five pounds on your shoulder. Look for a brand that has good worldwide service and a history of reliability. Look for strong construction and good service and stay with the major brands. Go with the machine that is comfortable for you, is light weight, has a long battery life, and has WIFI (Wireless Fidelity) or cloud capability.

If you go on a long-term outreach, it would be good to take the essential system CDs and/or backups of necessary data from "My Documents" from your computer. You may have to rebuild the hard drive in the event it needs to be reformatted. If it's not possible to take essential backups, you are at risk. If the system crashes due to a bug and it's not possible to recover, valuable records can be lost, critical communication ability can be crippled, and record-keeping tools can be lost. I recommend using a large capacity USB flash drive for backup. Your data can be backed up quickly and a flash drive will fit in your pocket or attached to a keychain for safe keeping.

It is important to backup data documents weekly or monthly at the longest. Once the initial backup is complete, only the new or changed items need to be backed up at that point. You can email important documents to yourself or to a seldom-used email address, one that is designated for safekeeping. Emailing important documents and leaving them on the Internet until they can be retrieved later is a trick I used to secure data when my computer was compromised. My hard drive was struggling, so I sent critical data to myself before I was forced to reformat the drive. I did not have a Flash drive available at the time. Also, e-mailing important documents to the support team at home is a good way to provide secure backup.

If you leave your computer system software at home and the system fails, you may be able to get a generic copy of the software reloaded in the field, but don't expect it to work like the original system software. Every computer manufacturer modifies Windows for their particular brand of computer. They have the software modifications needed for the brand and model of your computer. If in this situation, it may be possible to limp along until the branded software is available again.

Repairs in the field can be costly and finding a capable and qualified technician at a reasonable price can be a chore. Finding someone who speaks your language can be another challenge to write home about. An important thing to remember: If it takes an hour in the United States, it will take a full day in the foreign field. Sometimes it can be a most difficult thing just to accomplish the simplest task. It may require endless bus rides to technicians who are not qualified to repair your computer, but who are willing to try! If possible, try to go to a technician who is recommended by your local contact.

Taking a package of blank CDs can be a chore going through airports and riding on buses, but it is a lot easier than losing the services of the laptop because you could not back up the data. Take as much backup data as you need on one or more flash drives. They are easy to carry through airports, on trains or busses, or other transportation. Try to keep them attached to a key chain for more security.

Remember Murphy's Law: "If something can go wrong, it will." So be prepared and be as self-sustaining as possible. Don't take what is not needed, but do take what you need with a minimum of risk.

Never fear: lessons from life on a kibbutz

In 1998 and 1999, I was in Israel on summer outreaches with YWAM. We were working on a Kibbutz near Tel Dan, north of Galilee, south of Mt. Herman, and between the city of Kiryet Schmona on the east and the Golan Heights on the west. A kibbutz is a collective farm—a throwback to the old Soviet collective farms. This kibbutz was a factory that made rain boots.

Interestingly, the ordinary-looking men and women on the kibbutz were also members of the Israeli Defense Forces (IDF). They were tank drivers, machine gunners, and infantry, but they wore civilian clothes and worked in a boot factory. Some carried machine guns and it seemed like everyone had a weapon at hand. In case of national emergency, they were immediately on active duty and became a fighting unit. Kibbutz Dafna had been involved in many ongoing conflicts with the Muslims because of their location between Lebanon, Syria, and Jordan.

When the rocket alarms sounded, everyone had to immediately head for the bomb shelters scattered throughout the kibbutz. The Katusha rockets were fired from Lebanon or Syria into Israel, most of the time Kiryet Schmona and Kibbutz Dafna were the targets. We were less than 400 yards from the Lebanese border and probably less than four miles from the Syrian border, so we were within range.

We could hear the rockets coming because they gave out a characteristic whistle before they hit. A number of times the rockets got pretty close. On one occasion, they got within 200 feet of our small apartment. When they hit, they made large holes in the road, or the melon patch, or the tomato patch. Sometimes, when they aimed for Kiryet Schmona, the rockets passed over the city in the direction of the kibbutz. When the rockets came from Lebanon in the north, they were aiming directly for the kibbutz. When Kiryet Schmona was hit and there was loss of life, Israel would respond in kind to Lebanon or Syria. However, we never lost anyone on the kibbutz from the rockets.

When the alarm sounded and I was supposed to go to the bomb shelters, instead I headed for my room to send out emails asking for prayer. We did have a reinforced room in every apartment for shelter and sometimes I would send out prayer emails from the Safe Room. Sometimes I seemed to have time to send out prayer requests before I would hear the whistles.

There were several Kibbutzniks (residents of the Kibbutz) who became believers in Yeshuah (Jesus) while we were there. We could not expose their face to the rest of the people on the Kibbutz because the new believers would have been severely punished, but we were able to give them Bibles and we helped them in other ways while we were there. They would take their Bibles to the forest or farm where they worked to hide them from everyone. There they could read God's word in peace.

The moral of the story is: Never fear when the Lord is with you. The Lord is our shield and our protector, whom shall we fear?

Was I ever afraid? I can say I never was afraid. The thought just never occurred to me to be afraid, I was excited but not in fear. When the alarms went off, I had a job to do. I had to send a prayer request, to get them out by e-mail as soon as possible. That was my job for the Lord, and He took care of things after that.

Be alert to the feeling and needs of those around you

In 2005, I helped teach a counseling course at a Messianic Outreach Center in Tel Aviv, Israel, one night a week. A woman student from Norway always sat next to me and when she did, I would feel so sad I would almost be in despair. I just wanted to lie on the floor in emotional pain. I could not understand my feelings or my reactions and thought I was having a serious problem of some kind.

The leader of the counseling class and I talked about it, but there did not seem to be anything we could identify. One evening after class, the student and I talked on a personal level and I discovered her heartbreaking family situation back in Norway. Then I understood the Lord was allowing me to feel her pain.

I began praying into her situation and within two weeks it cleared up and she was delivered from the emotional pain of her tragic family situation. She was on the road to recovery and the Lord had allowed me to feel her pain, so I could intercede for her in prayer. That experience awoke me to the importance of prayer and intercession for our brothers and sisters in Christ.

A four question quiz that looks at your experiences

1. List some experiences that were hard, but through them, you learned valuable lessons.
2. List some experiences that were pleasant, and lessons you learned through them.
3. How have these experiences changed you? How has your character changed?
4. Are you in a learning experience at this time? What do you think the lesson will be?

Your Call to Missions

When you accept His call, your decision will have long-range consequences. A lot of preparations in time, energy, focus, and personal training will be forthcoming. However, God is investing in you too! He is investing His time, His energy, His training, and His focus in your preparation for ministry.

No two calls are alike, but there's a common thread in everything. The first common thread is perhaps a reluctance to accept the call. Many accept God's call immediately, but most of us do not. Fortunately, it does not matter whether we say "Yes" or "No," but rather what matters is what we actually *do*! Jesus asked the people:

> But what do you think? A man had two sons, and he came to the first and said, 'Son, go, work today in my vineyard.' He answered and said, 'I will not,' but afterward he regretted it and went. Then he came to the second and said likewise. And he answered and said, 'I go, sir,' but he did not go. Which of the two did the will of his father?—Matt 21:28-31a, (NKJV)

The first son said "No," but changed his mind and obeyed his father's request. The second son said, "Yes" but didn't do as he was asked. The first son, who actually did as he was asked, is the one who was obedient and honored.

It is okay to question the call on your life. You need God's confirmation and not just a presumption of His call. With His assurance, you will not waver when challenges or distractions come. Be secure in Him and His plan for your life. However, if you presume God's call, you will soon waver, and it's only a matter of time before you crash and burn spiritually. The ministry may suffer, and you may become a casualty in the process.

If the Lord is not calling you to service in an area, He will bring a detour because He may have another plan for you. Be open to this. What is important is your desire to serve Him. The enemy is aware of the call God has on your life, and he will try to distract you. For example, pride, self-interest, sin, or lack of commitment can be a detour, but do not fall for them. When you sense a focus in your life, do not be distracted from it.

The enemy can only offer an illusion of something better to distract you. Sometimes it's only a distraction to get your focus off your calling. Once he has distracted you, he stands a good chance of succeeding in his plan. If you do get distracted from your calling, and you realize it, repent and get back on track as soon as possible. Stay focused on God's plan. It's better to obey the Lord than to repent and have to pick up the pieces later:

> *"So Samuel said: Has the LORD as great delight in burnt offerings and sacrifices, As in obeying the voice of the LORD? Behold, to obey is better than sacrifice, and to heed than the fat of rams."*—1 Samuel 15:22 (NKJV)

What your call may sound like

God can call someone to missions in many ways, but His call will always be personal. It could be during an evangelistic crusade, a church campaign, or a still, small voice in the quiet of the evening. You may hear a casual word like, "Someday you will be a missionary." However He speaks to you, it will be personal. You will also have a sense of ownership in your heart, although you may not be able to explain it clearly.

One of the stages of discovering God's call on your life will be a focus or burden in your heart for a culture, a people, or language group. Perhaps a geopolitical area will fascinate you, and you will want to know more about it. It will be a growing curiosity that will rise above the normal. You will have a hunger to know more about your focus or burden. Perhaps you will also have a skill in ministry. It could even be a secular skill such as aircraft maintenance, piloting, a ships engineer, navigating, cooking, carpentry, administrative assistance, or any multitude of skills that are desperately needed and in short supply in a ministry, the mission field, or ministry in general.

I worked in the defense industry during the Cold War period and the Soviet Union was always the enemy. Consequently, I wanted to know as much as possible about Russia. I became fascinated with Russian history. I was able to read the New Testament in Greek so studying the Russian language was a lot easier for me since the Russian alphabet is based on the Greek alphabet. This helped me to read and speak the language easier than normal when I actually arrived in Ukraine and Russia. The Lord was preparing me. He used my desire and passion for Russian history to prepare me to live among the people.

The primary need for missionaries is to have a heart for people; this is the foundation of missions. It's all about reaching people with the Gospel, seeing them come to Christ and growing in the Lord. I've heard it said, "If it wasn't for people, ministry would be a piece of cake." But isn't that what it's all about?

A genuine call to missions brings a burden above the ordinary and it will be an on-going burden. When the Lord puts a burden or calling on your heart, it will not go away unless you say, "No." He will not force you to follow Him. The Lord may ask you to serve Him and if the answer is still, "No," someone else will get the blessing. The blessing will go to the one who says, "Yes" and does it.

This is illustrated from the book of Esther:

> *And Mordecai told them to answer Esther: Do not think*
> *in your heart that you will escape in the king's palace any*
> *more than all the other Jews. For if you remain completely*
> *silent at this time, relief and deliverance will arise for the*

*Jews from another place, but you and your father's house
will perish. Yet who knows whether you have come to the
kingdom for such a time as this?*

—Esther 4:13-14 (NKJV)

Think of this: are certain people a burden on your heart?
Do you have a focused interest in a certain area of ministry? If
the Lord puts these on your heart, they will stay there in your
thoughts, and over the long-term, your focus will move in that
direction. There will be a driving force to experience life and
ministry in your area of interest.

How do I know if I'm called? *(Hint: Pray)*

It is very important to pray about your calling and seek God's
confirmation. If God is speaking through the burden of your
heart, ask Him to confirm it, and when He does—accept it. Ask
Him to direct your path and prepare you for what He has for
you. He will remember your "Yes" answer, and He will begin
preparing you.

If you do not receive a recognized confirmation, then wait.
Not receiving an answer does not necessarily mean "No." It
may not be the right time. Keep on preparing to serve Him the
best way you know how. Be prepared for when the time comes.
However, remember to not move ahead of the Lord. He knows
where you live, and He will not forget you. At the right time,
He'll move in your life:

> *The hands of Zerubbabel have laid the foundation of
> this temple; His hands shall also finish it. Then you will
> know that the LORD of hosts has sent me to you. For
> who has despised the day of small things?*—Zechariah
> 4:9-10a (NKJV)

Do not despise the day of small things; big things start small.
The small things are your training to handle the big things.

Be faithful in the small things, and when God can entrust you with the bigger things, you will move on to the next step. When you are ready with faithfulness in ministry, and your skill and maturity have been proven in the small things, you will move on in ministry at the right time. He wants you to succeed, so He will prepare you to succeed.

There is too much at stake and souls will be depending on your stability. Times will get tough; you can count on that. There will be disappointment, discouragement, attacks from other Christians, and more. You must be strong in your faith, assured of your call, and unmovable under fire. If you do *not* move to higher levels of responsibility, don't worry about it. You could be right where God wants you. The important point is not to move ahead of the Lord, but to do exactly what He wants you to do.

King David started life as a shepherd boy, and the Lord Jesus began His ministry in a carpentry shop. Billy Graham did not start as a world-class evangelist; he started in a little country church and then moved up to a tent of all things! The army sends men through boot camp before they are given a gun. Boot camp is training for the big things to come so they will be prepared and ready. God will not give you ministry leadership until you are prepared to minister and able to lead. You have to go through boot camp training before God gives you ministry responsibility.

If one is called to be a Sunday school teacher all their life, they are blessed. It may not seem as exotic as going to New Guinea or far off lands, but remember, one of the mighty men of God, Dwight L. Moody, was led to the Lord in the shoe store where he worked with his Sunday school teacher. D.L. Moody became an evangelist who reached two continents for Christ. That obscure Sunday school teacher is an example of faithfulness and obedience to his calling, and he will share in D.L. Moody's reward.

D.L. Moody started at the bottom just like all of us. We progress from kindergarten, through all the grades, and through college and graduate school before we go into the real world of missions and ministry.

Billy Graham received Christ as his savior when he went to a gospel tent meeting led by Mordecai Ham, a traveling evangelist. Billy went there just to taunt the evangelist and had his life changed by the power of God. Think of these men who are faithful in the little things and how God multiplies the blessings into greatness. The Sunday school teacher and the evangelist led two men to Christ, one a shoe store clerk and the other a rebellious student. They in turn became world-class evangelists, responsible for millions being brought into the Kingdom of God. They started in humble beginnings and rose to their world-class calling. They did not do it alone. God called many faithful men and women to support them, and these supporters also share in the reward together.

Seek wise counsel and do research

Seek the counsel of a trusted pastor or older friend who has perhaps been on the mission field or retired from missionary service. Attend church or college mission conferences. Research your area of interest by writing to agencies or missionaries serving in that area. If possible, exchange pictures. Make yourself available for service in your church or with a local ministry in your community. This will add to your experience in service and servant-hood and prepare you for the mission field—or any field of ministry. This is a time of preparation, to explore and confirm God's call on your life and to prepare for your calling.

When you are researching mission agencies, prayerfully look at their ministry focus and the pros and cons of each agency. It is possible to do a lot of research on the Internet, but don't neglect direct contact with an agency. Apply to become a summer intern with an agency. A summer of service with a sending agency will expose you to their service specialty, and you will meet a lot of nice people for your effort. You will only be serving for a summer period, so don't worry about a long-term commitment unless the Lord brings you to this point. All experiences are ministry preparation and this summer experience will be a part of the overall ministry opportunities and experiences.

With today's high level of communication, telephone calls or emails anywhere in the world can be made with ease. However, be very aware that in some countries of the world it's not good and can even be dangerous to use religious "Christian" words. This can easily cause harm to resident missionaries or anyone even associated with the missionary. Be careful in these situations not to speak *Christianize*; try to substitute business or technical terminology, or even words in common usage to represent Christian meanings.

For written messages such as email, always clear the level of sensitivity in the words you use with the missionary. Another procedure would be to write to the sending agency, and they will screen the email for the resident missionary. They can then remove sensitive data and rewrite your letter using safe and acceptable terminology, and then they'll forward it to the person you are trying to contact. The missionary in turn may write back to the agency and the agency will translate the sensitive data and forward the email to you.

Sensitive information is any data that reveals names, locations, finances, ministry activity, or anything that could be used against the missionary or that might cause problems for the missionary in their place of service. The sending agency or the missionary will decide the level of freedom to use. Respect the wishes of the agency and missionary, otherwise communication will be stopped for the safety and security of the missionary and the ministry.

Sometimes in public or in an insecure place, you may need to cover your words with Mission Speak. For example, use such words as "CEO" or "Boss" to refer to the Father. The CEO is the Chief Executive Officer of a business and he runs the business. I've also used phrases like: "I'm going to talk to the CEO tonight," meaning I was going to pray to the Father tonight. I use "The Boss" to refer to the Lord.

On occasion I've identified myself as a "Yogurt M&M." This tells the person I'm a Missionary with Youth With A Mission

(YWAM). I might also say something like "Yogurt Larry will be here next week to talk about John," where "Larry" is with Youth With A Mission, and he'll be speaking about the Gospel of John. The word substitutes don't have to be rigid; you may want to vary them and on occasion change the agreed-on substitute word. These substitute words should be agreed upon within the circle of your coworkers. Don't use this indiscriminately; save it for when you need it. Your coworkers should recognize when you *start* using substitute words that there may be a need for caution in your conversation.

Check your motive

Is your motivation to serve the Lord or is there a personal agenda? Is your reason for serving something other than to serve the Lord? You can't serve the Lord as a life direction if you have any objective other than to just serve the Lord.

If the Lord is the Lord of your life, then He has the right to direct your life. If *you* are directing your life, there's a conflict! Some people will try to serve the Lord for money, power, prestige, family values, or acceptance from peers. Your motives will be challenged, and testing times will reveal your personal motives for what they are.

I have known missionaries that have served with a wrong spirit. They have had successful ministries in other fields back home, but in their overseas mission efforts they're an accident waiting to happen. One key to overseas or foreign missions is having a servant's heart. Serving overseas without a servant's heart is a recipe for disaster. Others can see the intent of your heart even when you cannot see it yourself.

I know a person who teaches with an international ministry who was asked to leave a mission outreach, to get out of the way, and not to bother the indigenous ministry. He went with a wrong spirit, a wrong attitude, and he didn't know the culture he was trying to minister to. What was acceptable back home had a negative effect overseas. He had a successful ministry in the

United States, but since he was not open to advice and counsel for ministering in another culture, so it didn't go well. Ministries suffer when people go unprepared and untrained for foreign ministry. A haughty spirit and being culturally unprepared to serve in a foreign culture can produce regrettable results.

If you get a rewarding feeling helping people in the nursing home, this may be a good indicator that perhaps this is the call God has on your life for this time. There is no applause or accolades ministering in a nursing home, but the joy of the Lord and His presence can be overwhelming and rewarding. If that's your motivation, go for it until He takes that joy of ministry away. Seek the Lord in prayer. It may be time to move on to the next venture in ministry, but wait for His confirmation. These experiences are all preparations for the next big step with the Lord. Each ministry experience adds to the foundation of your calling and your life experiences are a process of Christian growth. Each calling is for "such a time as this."

Do you have an interest in the mechanics of a sermon? This might indicate the Lord is leading you to the teaching or preaching ministry. In your preparation, He'll bring opportunities for you to learn speaking skills and will lead you to Bible College and seminary. Contact your pastor for counseling and direction.

Do you have a desire to stand up and tell everyone about Jesus? Perhaps your focus is in Bible teaching or evangelism. Are you bold enough to speak for Christ at school in spite of the attitude of others toward you? Perhaps the Lord's calling might be to serve in a Frontier Missions setting.

Is there an area of the ministry that is of particular interest to you? Follow your passions. I led a nursing home ministry for years, and I loved it. It drew to a close after several years, but everything I learned in this ministry was put to use in later years—in missions.

Here are some questions to consider. These questions are designed to help you discern God's call on your life. Pray into your focused area of interest.

1. Do you feel drawn to a people group, a geographic location, or a language group?
2. Is this a continuing feeling and do you feel purposeful in this calling?
3. Is your interest in long-term or short-term ministry, or are you exploring opportunities for your life direction?

Do you have the passion for ministry?

Do you feel a passion for a people group or a ministry? If you do not feel a passion for the ministry, or you do not feel a passion for a people group, you are probably not ready for a ministry or for missions.

No passion = No calling

The passion could be a focused interest or an overwhelming love for a people or ministry. This will be a driving force to move in a direction that leads to the destination God has called you to. There must be a sense of *calling* on your life even though you may not be able to see the long-range view. There must still be a sense of God's call on your life even though the ministry, people, or locations are not on your radar screen at this time. Your passion and drive will confirm this in your heart.

If you go on an outreach without a passion for ministry, it is only a vacation with a purpose. You can go into a ministry for the fellowship, camaraderie, or peer pressure but unless you have a passion for the ministry, it won't take long before you will experience burnout or people fatigue. If that happens, you will know you possibly made a hasty decision or that this outreach was not your area of calling. Allow God to use this as part of your growth experience.

If you find yourself in this situation, the way out is not to run from it, but to work through it. Begin every morning in the workplace with prayer. Pray the Lord will give you a love for the ministry, a love for the people, and a love for your work responsibility. Pray that the Lord will give you a passion for the situation you find yourself in. Pray *into* your situation. God has allowed this in your life for your personal growth experience, so don't lose this chance to grow.

This situation can be one of the most rewarding experiences of your life. You will experience personal growth and ministry growth in the tough times. Pleasant experiences do not allow for much personal growth. But difficult experiences can make us blossom.

Remember, God is training you for a ministry and this may be a boot camp experience. Get over it and learn all you can. Suck in the gut, Soldier of the Cross; you're being trained for the ministry. You are in the greatest, most powerful army of human history, and the battle and the war are real. You are being trained for spiritual combat, and the situation you are currently in is part of the training.

I hope this encourages you because it's true. I have been in this battle for over fifty years, and I'm still learning to be a soldier of the cross. One thing I've noticed: When you are successful over one obstacle or area of weakness, you do not have to repeat it. Otherwise the situation will repeat itself until you get it right! When you have the victory in a situation, you will find you have a *new* situation to conquer shortly after it. Your strength and maturity will be built one situation at time, one situation upon another until you are a mature warrior for the Lord.

Another word of wisdom: Pain is weakness leaving your body (that's an old Marine Corps word of encouragement), and it's the same in the Lord's Army. Personal pain is there to let you know you have a weakness and the Lord wants you to be like Him, whole and perfect. This situation is to strengthen you for a ministry. The Lord will focus on your weaknesses to make you strong. This is not for your hurt; it's for your good, so be strong in His might because He is strong.

Finally, my brethren, be strong in the Lord and in the power of His might.

—Ephesians 6:10 (NKJV)

Confirming your call

A wonderful way to begin exploring missions is to go on a weekend outreach. A good beginning is participating in an outreach with your home church or sister church. Start small and with whatever is comfortable for you, but be sure to allow room to stretch yourself. Start where you are and do not be afraid to extend your reach to find your limit. Don't be afraid to do something you have never done before. If an offer is brought to you, try it. This may be the Lord's way of allowing you to grow in ministry experience.

I never liked church outings or retreats, and I still don't. I have been in ministry since 1988 and in full-time missions since the 1993. I've been all over the globe from China to Israel, England, Russia, Ukraine, Hungary, and more, but I still don't like church retreats.

God will put a burden in your heart for the place or people of your calling. When I lived in Ukraine, chickens had been kept in my room up until a couple of days before I moved in. In fact, they moved the chickens out so I could have the room! Imagine what that smelled like! After a week or so, I couldn't even smell the chicken odor, and then it became quite a comfortable room for me.

I loved my little chicken room because I was called to missions and to the people of Eastern Europe. That's the difference: I was never called to a retreat ministry so even though the beds were okay, I never liked retreats. However, I really loved my little chicken room in Kiev, Ukraine, because I was called to minister to the people in Kiev, Ukraine. The moral: You will love where you are called and what you are called to do, no matter how unusual it is.

Did your outreach experience increase your appetite for more?

Did you sense God's hand in your outreach experience? Did you "see" Him at work there? If the answer is "Yes," you'll know the blessing and sense of fulfillment. God will bless all you do in serving Him, in the small things and the big things. If you didn't sense His blessings or satisfaction, perhaps you need to find out why. Maybe your sensor needs a tune-up or perhaps God is being silent for a reason. If He's being silent, try to find out why. A note here: the enemy will try to discourage you, so try to see if that could be a cause of any discouragement.

Whatever the reason for this situation, God will use this experience in your life for your good. God does not always respond with an "Atta-Boy" feeling, but sometimes it's just the peace of His presence that surrounds you. I have sensed His presence with me many times while abroad. I also sensed His presence with me in the nursing home ministry I led. I loved them all because they were where I was called for that season in my life for my training in ministry.

The Lord's presence in an outreach will be an empowering experience. You will feel good about yourself because of God's presence in the experience with you. There have been times when I acted on faith without the assurance of knowing what I was doing, and I didn't feel bold in ministry. Still, in those times the Lord was there and empowered me. He made the results turn out well. In fact, others thought I understood what I was doing even though I didn't have the assurance! It was God's hand at work all the time. The Lord honored my willingness to serve.

You may be asked to speak at a church and afterward not remember what you spoke about! You may even remember what you spoke about and feel you did a terrible job. The surprise will be when people may come to you afterward and tell you how blessed they were with your message! Then you will realize it's not about you, it couldn't have been you because it's about Him. It's not how eloquently you spoke, or how technically wonderful your message was (because it probably wasn't), but the Holy Spirit took your message and blessed people with His message. People may have thought it was you, but you will know the truth; it wasn't you. It's all about Jesus and it was God at work in your message.

If you decide to follow the Lord, He'll enable you to meet that call, and it'll be at the right time. The path may seem like a woven tapestry of experiences and some false starts, but He'll "get you to the train on time." He'll work out the circumstance to direct your path without the need for your planning. Planning is necessary, but the Lord is in control. Sometimes your plans will change and you will wonder why or how that happened. This is the Lord at work, redirecting your path. Don't worry; He's in command. Once you commit your way to Him, He'll direct your path, not you. He will let you get in the way sometimes, and if you're committed to Him, He will correct your path again.

Sometimes you won't have a clue about the things that are happening in your circumstances, but don't worry, He's still directing things. He may allow you to choose your own way and allow you to get led off track, but He's faithful to bring you back on track in your commitment to serve Him. For example, if you are late for something, you may see later it was good to have been late. There may have been an accident in your path if you had been on time! There will be a reason for the timing in all you do, but you probably won't see it until the event has passed, and it may actually be years later before you see what He was doing "way back then!"

One caveat here: The Lord will allow you to make a bad decision if your enthusiasm gets ahead of His plans for your life. The consequences of a bad decision may be painful and costly for you, but He will allow this experience for our personal growth and maturity. I have learned these experiences more times than I care to remember, but it seems every time I step off the path, I learn more about waiting on the Lord. The consequences have been painful physically, emotionally, and financially. But, through these experiences and God's correction, I've stayed on track in God's plan for my life. It would have been so much easier, and more beneficial for me, to have controlled my enthusiasm and zeal and waited for the Lord to move.

As an example, when I was invited to go skiing the Lord spoke to me several times not to go. I went skiing anyway and I had a bad ski accident. It took me over a year to recover and get back on track because the ski accident derailed me. That is just one example.

There is a law of unintended consequences. These are consequences that you could not see when you made a decision, which were hidden from view. He'll direct your path and help you choose the right way even though it will seem like you are making the decisions. Prayer is the key; stay in an attitude of prayer. God is faithful and He won't let you crash and burn. You may wonder about this sometimes, but in the end, you will still be on the right path.

I hunger for more life in the mission field. I can't seem to get much passion worked up for a jaw-dropping golf score or eating at a new restaurant. Living in my home culture lacks the dynamic life of the mission field where the Father is working, is alive, and is dynamic!

Imagine how rewarding it is to learn a new language at the street level, to be able to hear and understand, to speak and be understood, and to be able to read books of another culture, and in their language. This will open new worlds of communication and understanding for you. In general, it will take a few years to gain a working knowledge of a new language.

If you're living in the culture you're called to, learning the language and customs of the people will seem comfortable, exciting, and personally rewarding. It may be hard and you may wonder if you can do it. One day, though, it will all come together and you will have a sense of being at home with the people. You will fit into your surroundings and the presence of the Lord will be your companion and guide.

If this is not your calling, you won't feel at home unless the Lord gives you the grace to live there. If He gives you the grace to forbear, and this may only be for a season, you will be rewarded with His presence because of your obedience. You may be holding the fort until a special person arrives to take over, and your faithfulness to obey will have been critical.

Much of the ministry of foreign missions involves relocation for periods of time, so you may be outside your targeted culture, or people group, or comfort zone for a season. This could be due to visa renewal, R&R trips, ministry opportunities in neighboring countries, and other reasons. R&R can be Rest and Recovery, Rest and Redirection, or Rest and Relaxation—whatever fits the need of the situation.

Living in your culture or people group, you will likely fit in eventually, regardless of what difficulties exist at the time. However, even though it may take years to "fit in," you will still have a sense of knowing that you're called to these people. Not all calls are for a lifetime, so look at every calling for a season. When you lose the sense of belonging and the grace to remain there, the season may be over.

When this happens it may be time to go back home, or wherever you call home, for a season of rest. Losing a sense of belonging does not mean the end has come to the involvement in missions. It may be for a season of rest and/or it may be the beginning of a new venture with the Lord. When the right time comes, the Lord will direct your path elsewhere, but don't be hasty to start in a new direction.

Do not enter your calling in a hurry, and do not leave your calling in a hurry. Never make a choice in a vacuum. Always rely on your prayer partners. There's an old saying: "Act in haste and you'll repent in leisure." In other words, if you act in haste, you may spend a long time getting out of a situation made from the hasty decision.

If it's a new venture, you'll build on your prior life experiences. The rest and recovery may last several weeks to several years, but it will allow you to recharge your physical and spiritual batteries. You can use this time for fund-raising, building friendships, creating/growing support teams, continuing education, or just resting in the Lord. The Lord may even remove you from a ministry for a season, perhaps for a needed vacation before He redirects your path.

Missions will be addictive or terrifying

It seems to me like missions is life; personally, I don't have a strong identity outside of missions. It's who I am. I'm very happy with this and I cannot imagine doing anything else. I've tried other things and found nothing else gives me the peace of mind, personal satisfaction, and sense of fulfillment as serving the Lord in missions. I tried to leave missions several years ago and floundered for four years with no direction and no job satisfaction. Just how exciting can you get over a good bowling score, a killer golf score, a new movie, or going fishing? Yuck.

Missionary service is dynamic, exciting, fulfilling, and—best of all—the Lord's presence is there! Ministry is challenging and rewarding. Meeting fellow believers in foreign lands, with a common bond of Christ, is an exhilarating moment in life!

This is quite true and you will discover it pretty quickly too. If you feel unsettled or somewhat terrified, don't worry about it; it doesn't mean you're a bad person. The mission field is only for those called to the mission field. Don't feel you're a failure or rejected if you are not called to missionary service. It's just that this may not be God's best for you, or it may not be where He's called you at this time. It may be just a passing interest, and He wants you to know something about it for the next step of growth in your life.

You will know quickly if a mission experience was part of a long-term plan for you. It may be the Lord has called you to another field of service, or with another agency, and this experience is only a part of the preparation for your long-term call. This experience will be for building faithfulness as will all of life's experiences. We benefit and grow personally in everything we do with the Lord. Where we go and what we do are only part of the personal growth experience He has for each one of us.

In my ministry experience, I have been called to a different field of service every couple of years. I have been called to Ukraine, Russia, China, England, the United States, and Israel. I keep growing in the Lord as education, training, and life skills grow. And you will grow more with every adventure the Lord has for you, in ways you could never have otherwise imagined. Some missionaries are called to one field of service and that may never change, but every call is different and the Lord will lead you with a personal calling.

Call to missions questionnaire

This little questionnaire will give a measurable yardstick to help you see if there's a call on your life to missions. Think about the questions and answer them as accurately as possible.

Choose (0) Not true
   (1) Sometimes true
   (2) Mostly true
   (3) Definitely true

a. *Do you enjoy the company of those of different racial, economic, or ethnic backgrounds, and do you feel accepted by them?*
   (0) (1) (2) (3)

b. *Do you have the desire to learn a different language in order to minister to those in a different culture?*
   (0) (1) (2) (3)

c. *Are people of different races and ethnic cultures attracted to you and do you relate well to them?*
   (0) (1) (2) (3)

d. *Are you willing to leave the conveniences and comforts of home if it would enable you to share Christ with more people?*
(0) (1) (2) (3)

e. *Do you desire to see people of other countries won to the Lord perhaps more than those in your own neighborhood?*
(0) (1) (2) (3)

Total your score and grade yourself from 0 to 15. The higher your score the more assured you can be that you have a future in missions.

1. *If you scored less than 5* you should probably not think of missions as a career choice at this time.

2. *If you scored between 5 and 10,* you're a candidate, but don't rush into it, this may not be the right time.

3. *If you scored over 10,* you're on your way and you need to focus your prayers to seek ministry opportunities.

4. *If you hit 15,* you're well on your way in God's calling on your life, so start making serious preparations.

Evaluating Your Call

Be sure the Lord has called you to serve Him because your commitment will be tested. You can expect opposition. When you're being tested, it will seem like those closest to you will be your strongest critics, even well-meaning Christian friends and family. God wants the best for you and others will want the best for you too. What your friends and family want for your life may not be God's best for your life. If your friend's logic makes sense but is opposed to what your heart says is God's call on your life, it is always better to follow God's call for your life. Involve your prayer partners and/or support team in your decision and commitment because they will confirm God's call in your life.

God will put the desire in your heart for a people group or geographic location. Go with your heart and don't necessarily look for a sign or a fleece, so to speak. Gideon used a fleece of wool in Judges 6:36-40 to determine God's will for him. He first asked God for dew on the fleece and to leave the threshing floor dry, and a second time he asked God to make the fleece dry and the threshing flood damp. Signs and fleeces may work for you but let Spirit's guiding in you be the final judge. I don't know anyone who looks at fleeces with any reliability.

The enemy senses God's call on your life and your commitment and will challenge you. You can count on it. He'll attack through finances, friends, and fatigue to discourage you. He'll attack in areas of perceived weakness. He'll try to convince you that you only *thought* you were called to missions, but you were never *really* called to missions. In addition, if you're called to missions the enemy may offer you a title, a promotion, a raise, or a spouse to divert you; whatever it is that can possibly distract you. Do not be fooled by the temporal. God's best for you is *the* best for you.

Networking and core team building

Do not try to work independently; there is strength in wise counsel. Start building a prayer and support team, and building accountability into your team. This will keep you focused and accountable for the long haul. Your prayer and support teams are on your side. Meet with them regularly, monthly if possible, to review your progress as a team. Build a team spirit in your selected partners because in the spirit, your partners will be going to the mission field with you.

Begin building a mailing list of potential prayer partners and financial supporters. This is called networking and multiplying the team. It costs money to go to the mission field, and you have to depend on support finances to pay the bills. You'll also need prayer partners to survive the spiritual battles that will come your way. Prayer partners are the other half of your support team.

As you build your support team and begin networking and raising funds, develop a regular newsletter mailing. The purpose is to develop relationships for support and prayer partners. This will be a good exercise in developing networking skills that you will need on the mission field and in ministry later.

I recommend a mailing and support database called TntMPD. This software is written by Campus Crusade for Christ International, or Cru, (CCC) and it's written by missionaries specifically for missionaries. I have used it for years and it is user friendly, it is free, and CCC provides excellent support. The web address is www.tntware.com or you can also contact them at www.CCC.org. They offer TntMPD to ministries for a freewill offering.

Researching your target people group

God may put a specific people group or geographic location on your heart. When you sense this, focus your prayers into this goal. Seek God's confirmation and involve your prayer partners all along the way. Wait to see where He takes you before you move in that direction. He will be faithful to ease you in the right direction. However, He may also lead you in another path for a while, so don't get confused if your path goes in an apparently different direction. Keep your focus and see if the indirect path may be part of the preparation in the short-term for your true calling in the long-term. Make a journal of your discoveries and conclusions for future reference. This will be a big help in raising funds as you can speak from your own experiences.

As a research tool, the web provides a wealth of online resources. Visiting a local library for resource information can be a good starting point. Examine a world map or a map of the specific country, including city maps. Familiarize yourself with the country and its cities, and orient their locations and relationship to each other. Study the language, religion, geopolitics, and cultural history as far back as possible. This will give you an understanding of the spirit and the ruling principalities over the country. Document your research and prepare a report for your prayer and support team in preparation for fund-raising.

I was fascinated with Russia and Russian history for a long time. I worked on military contracts for the government for years, and Russia was America's enemy at that time. I wanted to know more about them, so I studied their history back to the 6th century from a book I got from the U. S. State Department. I was also interested in Bible translations so I studied Greek. I wanted to know why there were different Bible translations and which translation was the most accurate and closest to the original language. I learned they are all good, even though some are more reliable or accurate translations for today's common use language.

When I was preparing to go to Ukraine, I was surprised to learn the primary language was Russian and the Russian language is based on the Greek alphabet. So my studies in one language area (Greek) applied to my calling in another language area (Russian). Being able to read Greek helped me understand the

Bible and even helped me learn Russian enough to function in the land of my calling. I love the Russian people to this day and I still think their history is fascinating.

I've heard very favorable reports about two language learning systems, www.RosettaStone.com and www.Pimsleurapproach.com. I've found them to be premium language learning resources with a consistent level of excellence. Learning the language of your target country is an investment in your preparation and will enhance your effectiveness in whatever you do.

You can do a lot of research on the Internet mostly free. This will probably be one of your best resources to start with without leaving home. If you can use your computer to research a language and learn to speak a few practical phrases, you will gain an immense advantage and an advanced understanding of the heart of the people when you finally are in country.

If it's possible, take a vacation to the country you are researching. Or you may want to try a short-term outreach of a week or two with your church or some other trustworthy group—one that has a good history in short-term outreaches. If you feel a call to a specific area, it may be possible to go with a small group of interested friends to that area in a prayer journey. On the home front, cultivate relationships with associates who have a similar interest. Perhaps you can persuade them to accompany you in a surveying trip to your desired country.

You should develop two teams: your support team back home and a team on the mission field. Keep your home support team aware and knowledgeable of your in-country team's fellowship as it develops. Include your support team partners back home in all you do.

Church denominations have organized short-term outreaches that are well-supervised for your safety. If this appeals to you, it can be a good experience. If it's not a good experience for you, then maybe you need to reconsider your call or perhaps this particular adventure was not where the Lord has called you. Good or bad, you will learn from it; think of it as "eating the meat and spitting out the bones."

God will use this experience to prepare you for the next step. So if you find this outreach was not what you expected, it will still add to your experience with the Lord, and you'll have gained an immense amount of personal growth and maturity. Keep seeking God's call on your life, He'll reward you openly and use every experience for your good. Once you find God's place for you, all of your previous experiences, good or bad, will come into play, and you'll see just how especially God has been at work in your life, preparing you for this day.

Paying the price

What price can it be that Jesus hasn't already paid for your victory!

> *I have been crucified with Christ; and it's no longer I who live, but Christ lives in me; and the life, which I now live in the flesh I live by faith in the Son of God, who loved me and gave Himself up for me.*—Galatians 2:20 (NKJV)

If you are called to missions, you will pay a personal price. I became aware of this after several years in missions. When you are committed to God's calling, your commitment will be challenged. The enemy seems to know where you live, and he will try to bring discouragement and diversion into your life to lead you away from your commitment. However, God will use what the enemy brings into your life to give you strength and develop character, peace, and patience. The enemy's attack is not always with bad things; sometimes it is a good thing, even a beautiful thing. However, the result will be to lead you away from your commitment to the Lord. God will bring you the right thing when you need it and it will be good.

When I was a new believer I use to pray for patience. I did this for at least a year and I couldn't believe all the awful stuff that was happening to me. Then one day, I was reflecting on a situation and I noticed how I was demonstrating a lot of patience. I laughed when I realized God had been bringing these situations into my life in answer to my prayers for patience. God is faithful to answer our prayers. However, I don't pray for patience anymore. I think I have enough.

For I know the thoughts that I think toward you, says the LORD: thoughts of peace and not of evil, to give you a future and a hope Then you will call upon Me and go and pray to Me, and I will listen to you—Jeremiah 29:11-12 (NKJV)

Two direct attacks were aimed at me. One was a serious skiing accident that almost killed me and the other was in my prosperous financial situation. I mentioned the ski accident earlier. It was a hurtful attack. The other attack happened a few years later. I was involved in investing in the stock market, and I was prospering in an amazing way. I couldn't make a bad decision. Every decision I made brought me huge gains. It was truly intoxicating.

Since I was living overseas and thought I was a hot shot in the stock market, I let a trusted Christian stockbroker handle my account. He proceeded to churn my account—to buy and sell my portfolio to make his commissions. I lost almost everything before I decided to do something about it. When I arrived back in the states, thoughts of revenge were prominent in my mind, but I consciously decided by force of will to give this financial situation to the Lord and let Him deal with it. After all, I was still alive and I had much of my health back as the Lord had sustained me through the skiing accident. It was a terrible financial loss for me, but I'm still walking with the Lord today and serving Him instead of being in prison for acting out in anger.

At one time, I was on staff with Youth With A Mission, helping to staff a Discipleship Training School. In this course, every one of the students was challenged and one quit in the middle of classes. This was sad because even if she was not called to a long-term involvement in missions, the training she would have received could have become a lifetime of blessing.

Do not quit because the going gets rough; it will get rough. Expect it. The only time to worry is if it does *not* get rough, or you quit. Challenges to your commitment are part of the training for ministry. When you're on the mission field in a foreign culture and there is no support group to cheer you on, you have to be able to keep on going and not quit. Lives depend on your stability under fire. Besides, once the enemy knows the Lord is your strength and your strength is strong, he will have no power over you.

We're in a spiritual battle, and it's a war. Soldiers have to be trained to stand under fire; our armor is to protect us from the front, not the back. The military has boot camp to train soldiers for battle, and ministry training is your boot camp experience; to train you to be mature and strong for the spiritual warfare later.

One of the challenges to your call may be to say goodbye to your girlfriend or boyfriend to answer God's call on your life. This can be very traumatic and if it's a question of following God's calling or your emotions, I can tell you without hesitation to follow God's calling. Following the Lord is much more fulfilling than a lifetime of regret, wishing you had followed Him. Following Him will bring all the right things into your life anyway, including the right person for you! As the prophet Samuel records, "It's better to obey than to sacrifice."

> *The plans of the diligent lead surely to plenty, but those of everyone who is hasty, surely to poverty.*—Proverbs 21:5 (NKJV)

You may have to be willing to release the love of your life in following the Lord. His love must be number one. No person can take the place of the Lord.

In my own life, I have had to give up several deep emotional attachments. But if I had followed those relationships, I wouldn't be where I am today in God's plan for my life. I would probably be hustling bagels in a corner coffee shop on Staten Island, New York, instead of sharing my experiences in world missions.

For many people, God has a special person for them, and that person will fit right into His calling. It won't be an either/or choice.

I've known of a couple where one partner was called to missions and to a specific country but chose to marry instead. She spent a lifetime wishing she had chosen differently. Her children answered her call to missions and to the country she had been called to. This is good for the children, but how sad for that woman. She lived to regret it all her life. It does show God's faithfulness even when we do not choose His best for our lives.

I've also known many who met on the mission field or in Bible College, and they are walking together through life in a ministry as husband and wife. Along those lines, I don't know anyone who regretted waiting for God to bring the one He has chosen for them. Further, I don't know anyone who regrets serving the Lord. A hasty decision or an unwise choice can lead to a lifetime of regret. How important it is to have a solid prayer and support team behind you who can help you in making the right decision!

I know couples who have come from divorced situations, recommitted their lives to Christ, and then met their spouse on the mission field. God is blessing them and blessing their ministry in a powerful way. Divorce is not some unpardonable sin; God can use those involved in a fresh and mighty way.

Strength in Solitude

Your journey may be a lonely path. This isn't the norm for everyone and your call to singleness may only be for a season. There will be times of short- or even long-term singleness, but God's best for you is to have a partner who is called to compliment you and support you in your ministry calling. God has your entire life in view and you do not; you have to rely on Him to direct your path. It's like walking blindfolded: He is telling you to walk left or right or go straight. As long as you hear His voice you will be okay. If you get to a point where you cannot hear His voice, you will make a bad choice and stumble. This will be time to remake your relationship with the Lord and His grace.

God has your best interests on His heart and mind, and He can see your life from the beginning to the end. Trust Him and His best will be your life story. If God has called you, He has decided that you are the right person for His calling. Trust His judgment. Do you need a lot of emotional support or can you keep going when you're under pressure—with no friends to cheer you on?

Strength in Responsibility

You will have to be a proactive self-starter to accomplish the tasks you are sometimes called to perform. It goes with the territory. It is not the norm but on occasion it may be necessary. Can you be the one who slips into the position getting the job done without being asked? There may be no one else willing to do the work, but it still has to be done. Many times you will find there is no one else to share the load and you have to do it just to get the job done. Help is vital but you will have to be willing to do it without help until you can train others in the work of the ministry.

Sometimes you will be the one who catches the odd things that others happen to miss. You must be counted on to get the job done and see it through to completion. You cannot be a quitter even when the day is long and the help has all gone home and the task is still not done. This is when maturity pays off. If you are in charge, you are responsible. You must be able to do the work of the ministry before you can train and lead others.

You should be able to give credit to someone under you for a job well done. Do not be a controller—you cannot do it all and the Lord does not expect you to. Being a controller is not in His plan for you. Sometimes you have to do it all, but do not get stuck in this position as you will burn out. Also, you may be robbing someone else of the opportunity God has planned for them to grow in ministry. Give them the opportunity to grow. Train others and allow them to experience their God-given destiny. Know your boundaries and allow people to grow and mature, but be the assurance person, making certain a job is done well. And do not blame others if the work isn't accomplished—just get in there and help them do it. This is a mentoring approach to training them for leadership. People will be watching you as a leader and follower of Jesus Christ. You represent Him and are His embodiment on earth.

Can you be an encourager to those who are trying to do well but sometimes fall short? Do not carry the whole responsibility for the ministry. The more you are able to assign tasks to others, the more others will grow and the easier your job will be. Do not build a ministry empire you cannot walk away from. This is God's work anyway. People make mistakes, and it will be your job to walk them through their mistakes so they can grow through the experience. That's how we all grow.

Your training includes being comfortable as a servant and being willing to take no personal glory for the accomplishments of others or the group. Can you fade into the background and let lesser-qualified people get credit for the work you supervised? This is an act of training others for responsible leadership under your ministry. Do not take credit for someone else's accomplishments and do not give credit where it's not due to those under you. Others will respect you for your integrity if you follow this guide.

Can you rejoice when the work of the ministry is done well, even if you did not do it? This is important because if you are trying to do everything yourself, you are heading for burnout. The ministry is not yours to start with; it's the Lord's work, and it's His ministry. Excellence in ministry is the goal and your excellence and integrity will be replicated in those you are mentoring.

Be an encourager. Much of the ministry is either being trained or training others or encouraging and affirming them.

People are willing to help, and they will do a good job if someone is willing to train them and affirm them when they do well and not chastise them when they fail to do a good job. If they feel they can try and be safe if they fail, they will try, and try again. If you trust them, they will trust you.

If the ones you are mentoring or training show less initiative and energy than you, I believe their commitment is lacking and you should back away. Those in training must show more initiative or energy to learn than you are using in training them. Their energy level should demonstrate an eagerness to learn and a commitment to the ministry. Your time and energy are valuable—so do not waste it on those who are not committed.

Am I able?

You may not feel adequately prepared for a mission venture. The thing is, it is not about you and it is not about how you feel—it's about Him! The Lord will direct your life. A note here: Your adventure with the Lord will always be a step of faith. You may not always have the assurance you would like. Sometimes it will feel like stepping out of an airplane without a parachute, at an unknown altitude, and the Lord simply says, "Trust me." That is not comfortable but it is an imperative.

The ministry is God's work, and you are a valued helper; you are a worker in the Lord's vineyard. Rejoice that He allows you to be a part of what He's doing. So what part is it you can take credit for? The fruit of the ministry is His because He's the one who gives the growth. So do not try to take personal credit for the success of the ministry. Feeling prepared can sometimes be a way for us to try to take credit away from God.

You are called to plant the seed and add some fertilizer, water the plants, and occasionally get to pick some fruit. You are blessed to see the fruit of your ministry, and you may also see fruit from others who have gone before you. Just rejoice for the privilege of serving the King.

Stepping Out in Faith

As you believe for the greater things and act in faith, stay within the bounds of common sense. If you get outside the limits of common sense, you may get hurt, and it may be costly to you and the ministry. Remember: There is power to move mountains in God's Word, but there is no power in your words. We proclaim His Word and, in this, there is life and power.

You can step off a tall building in faith, believing you will float to the ground, but God has declared that gravity will bring you down at a very high rate of speed. Common sense says you are going to hit the ground in a hurry, and it'll hurt. God cannot save you from willful stupidity if you persist in making decisions of personal "faith" alone. Faith alone is not enough. We need faith *in*. Having faith that gravity will not kill you is foolish. We have to put our faith in something reliable—faith *in* God.

15 questions to help clarify your direction

1. *When did you first sense God's call on your life?*
2. *Is God's call on your life clear and well defined, or is it ambiguous and just seems like a vague general call?*
3. *Do you have a willingness to serve, but just can't seem to find your direction?*
4. *How have you sensed God's call?*
5. *Does a certain people group interest you? What's on your heart?*
6. *Is there a language that interests you or challenges you?*
7. *Is there a country that you feel drawn to? Why?*
8. *Is there a specific ministry that interests you?*
9. *Have you prayed into the feelings of your heart and has God responded to you?*
10. *Have you counseled with anyone?*
11. *Name people you consider to have wise counsel. Prioritize this list according to those most likely to enter into a counseling relationship with you.*
12. *What's your passion?*

13. *List the ministry experiences you've had, to date, in chronological order. Look for a pattern of training development with increasing ministry responsibility and then mark each item as good, bad, or neutral.*
14. *List those experiences you'd like to repeat and why.*
15. *What have you learned about ministry that you can build on?*

A Plan to Help You Get Started

Preparation may take years as you grow and mature in Christ, so do not be in a hurry. Enter into missions slowly and exit missions slowly. There are no shortcuts to maturity and there are no shortcuts to growth in Christ. Actually, it is a life-long process of personal growth, so enjoy the ride!

Preparation

When you decide to serve the Lord in missions, the Lord will begin to direct your path to the field He has for you. You may not notice much of a change at first but soon you will notice changes in your thoughts and desires that will seem to be quite natural to you. These changes may be ever so subtle. You will begin to feel uncomfortable with old habits and old ways that perhaps have been with you for a long time, or what you think has been a long time.

You may or may not like some of the things that will begin to happen in your life mysteriously and "for no reason." He will use those unpleasant moments to build a character change in you. In addition, your friends will notice a change in your choices, your habits, or your life before you are aware of a change.

I cannot remember growing in character by too many good experiences in my life. It seems like I learned how to handle a situation because the Lord previously put me in a similar situation, under stress, for training so when the real thing occurred later in life, I could deal with it in a Godly way.

Do not be surprised when you find yourself in the middle of a situation that you were drawn into and cannot seem to get out of. An example might be that you are accused of wrong-doing by a member of your board to the pastor, and it is total and complete fabrication because of a jealous board member of the opposite sex. I have experienced this situation in real life. It was completely fabricated fiction and was meant to harm my character. However, the senior pastor never lost faith in me and stuck by me. I noticed this has occurred several times and each time I was accused of something, the accusations and the accuser or accusers faded away. God allowed this accusation for my spiritual growth, but they hurt me personally every time.

The servant is not greater than his master. Jesus was unjustly accused, lied about, and called derogatory things, so it is fair to say you can expect the same treatment, my friend. Count it a privilege to be treated this way. Remember, people can accuse you all day long, but if you are right before the Lord, you will be vindicated. Even if it takes years to see that—as it has for me in the past.

Your life experiences are important

You are learning to follow Him, so learn all you can from the small experiences that are brought your way. God is bringing into your life those things you need to make you the person He wants you to be. I guess you could call it "a makeover." You'll need to be the right person for the job when you reach your calling. For example, how do you deal with a situation on the mission field when you are called on to judge a person's character by their action? You will need prayer and Godly wisdom to judge wisely. Affirm everyone involved and bring the situation to the cross. Practice makes perfect and training will pay off. Perhaps your Godly wisdom will save a person in ministry or a ministry itself. Your personal life experiences and spiritual growth will come into play.

How will I know where to go?

The most important thing you can do is pray and wait for the Lord to answer your prayers. Notice I said "prayers." That's plural. Continue in prayer until you see the Lord move in a certain direction and then follow Him in that direction. There may be many directions open for you. He will begin by opening opportunities where you are, perhaps in your church as a Sunday school teacher, or by becoming involved in the worship service, or in a church outreach to the community. These are all learning experiences. Through them you will begin to grow in your ministry preparation and become more involved. It may seem scary along the way, but as you grow and mature in experience, you will feel comfortable in ministry activities.

The Lord's direct leading may develop as an increased interest in a people group, ministry, or even continuing your education. Following the Lord when your interests increase would be exploring your interest in whatever direction you feel led and releasing any other opportunities from your radar screen.

Do not seek the Lord in circumstances. First seek confirmation in your heart for a direction and circumstances will follow. Ask the Lord for peace in the direction He has for you, and ask Him to take away the peace for the way He does not want you to go.

Look for circumstances or people that will be related to your prayers. This is hard to define because the circumstances or people may not be the same, but they may be similar each time. Try to be sensitive to the Holy Spirit and allow Him to direct your path. Keep alert for signs such as a blocked path or paths that seem to fade away and listen to your heart.

The Lord will put it on your heart and you will sense a focus to your calling. You will sense a burden that will not leave you. The right direction will remain open, and you can be sure you are *not* called to ministry or missions because it will be a closed door. A closed door will be one you cannot open. It will not open for you, so leave it alone and move on.

Try to form a support group of core people who will be your prayer partners and one person who will eventually become your forwarding agent. (Refer to the Section 9 for further information on *Forwarding Agents*.)

Establish a habit of regular monthly meetings for bonding time. Meet more often as needed, if only for fellowship and a meal to share your heart. This is a time of team building. Your team will help you discern God's call on your life and help you see the way. Build trust in your support team. You cannot put too much energy into the things you do to build trust and commitment with the team. They will be your lifeline when you are away.

The best way to prepare for ministry service is education and training. Going to the mission field, wherever and whenever that may be, will take years of personal preparation in servant-hood, education, ministry, and cross-cultural training. It's a lifetime journey and it starts when you finish this book.

When an older person goes to the mission field, their preparation has been in their life experiences, in the crucible of life. Many people outside of the United States seem to have an elevated respect for older people. This gives the older person favor with the people and their age earns them the right to be heard. It will also open many doors for ministry and friendship evangelism that may not otherwise be open.

Raising Funds

It takes at least a year or more to raise adequate support for the mission field. This is not a part-time job; it's the primary focus of your year. Think it's easy? It can be quite stressful and frustrating. Your support team should be meeting once a month on your behalf for prayer, newsletter preparation, and to manage your affairs. You should have a minimum of one hundred fifty people on your mailing list, but anything over that is better. A list of over two hundred will assure you of adequate financial support—as well as considerable prayer support.

I know one person who has over eight thousand people on his mailing list. He gets good support and he needs it as the leader of an international ministry. Your support team should be responsible for your monthly newsletter creation and distribution. They are the ones who will mobilize your prayer and financial support partners on the home front. Typically, you, as the missionary, write the rough draft of your newsletter, and your team will edit and publish it for printing and mailing.

For long-term ministry flexibility and ease of mobility, set up your financial support processing with a 501(c)(3) authorized ministry organization outside of your sending ministry. A sending agency is an agency that has 501(c)(3) tax status authorized to process your support with tax deductible receipts, so having an outside agency such as your church or other organization process your support will allow you to change sending agencies or fields of service without disrupting your support partner base. It will ease any interruption that might result from a change in your ministry. Some people will forget your support when you change sending agencies or fields of service. This can be disruptive on the field or cause your support to dry up.

When I was in Ukraine and Russia in 1995, I was told my support was only about fifty percent of the goal I was given to raise. As a result, I couldn't stay in-country and had to return home to raise additional funds. The sending agency in Colorado Springs, Colorado, processed all our support. I was able to raise additional support, but was told I still had not reached my goal. As a result, I had to leave the ministry. When I left, I went on staff at a church in Hillsdale, Michigan, for a pastor I'd known for several years. A short time later, I went with another mission agency, Youth With A Mission, in Virginia.

Six years later, in December 2001, I was visiting my sister in New York for a short while. She mentioned having sent several significant gifts for my support. She had also been receiving numerous appeal letters from the vice president of the ministry. He had been continuously sending appeal letters to her ever since she began sending support for me. She showed me the receipts. I told her I had not received any support from her. I was surprised at the strength of the letters she received and this raised my suspicion. I contacted the sending agency and asked for a full report of my support for 1994 and 1995 even though it was five years before.

When I received the records, they revealed I had received support from several churches and individuals in Michigan and Florida. I had no knowledge of their support so I was unable to thank them for it at the time. The support my sister sent in for me was credited to the vice president of the ministry. Nothing she sent in for me came to me. There were more churches and individuals in Florida who had the same experience. How's that for accounting practice? Who knows where this support went? It certainly did not come to me. Your support team should monitor your financial support closely and with all diligence continue to follow-up every donation with a thank you note if at all possible.

If you are already on the mission field and want to change sending agencies, problems can easily occur if your sending agency is processing your support. You will have to go through the process of disconnecting from your sending agency and reconnecting with the new sending agency. This takes time and it's not convenient. You will lose support if only for the transition period. People may also drop support thinking you are changing ministry focus or they may continue to send support to your old agency and not to your new sending agency. Or they may just fall off your support list never to be heard from again. If your support team processes your support, there will be no problems in changing agencies or fields of service.

Financial support will take care of your temporal needs on the mission field and your prayer team will provide the spiritual covering that will get you back home safely. Write your newsletters to your administrative support team and task them with printing and distributing your newsletters to prayer partners and support partners. It will be much easier to ask for prayer support than to ask for financial support. However, your support team will get your newsletter into the hands of the right people who will support your spiritual covering and financial support needs.

Start where you live

In Jerusalem, Judea, Samaria, and then to the world

> *But you shall receive power when the Holy Spirit has come upon you; and you shall be witnesses to Me in Jerusalem, and in all Judea and Samaria and to the end of the earth.*—Acts 1:8 (NKJV)

The biblical example of Acts 1:8 is to wait for God's enabling, then start in Jerusalem (your home base), to Judea (your neighborhood), Samaria, (your people group, region, or nation, etc.), and then all the earth. This applies to ministry, raising support, training, and just about everything in a ministry. Start where you are, in the situation you are in, and go from there. This is God's way of growth.

Mission agencies: A short list

All ministries listed here have given permission to be included in this book and all related text has been approved by these ministries.

1. Mission Resource Directory

The central directory of directories (a place to start your search), with groupings by subject, name, language, people, geopolitical identity, type of ministry, and events, with other directories and resources listed. This site is a wealth of information.

http://www.mrd.org

2. World Christian Resources Directory

The purpose of this web site is to provide information and resources on how you can reach your world for Jesus and other useful information for Christians. This web site provides information on resources in many different languages. The resources are listed in alphabetical order.

www.MissionResources.com

3. Oscar

The UK based information service for World Missions and a vacancy agent sponsored by Interserve. If you're involved or interested in missions or Christian work around the world, OSCAR is your gateway to useful information, advice, and resources. Categories are listed by Opportunity Zone, Service Zone, and Supporter Zone including events and related news about missions.

If you're involved or interested in world mission or Christian work around the world, OSCAR is your gateway to useful information, advice and resources.

http://www.oscar.org.uk/index.html

4. Youth With A Mission (YWAM)

Youth With A Mission is an international volunteer movement of Christians from many backgrounds, cultures and Christian traditions, dedicated to serving Jesus throughout the world. Also known as YWAM (pronounced "WHY-wham"), the purpose is simply to know God and to make Him known.

When YWAM began in 1960, our main focus was giving young people opportunities to demonstrate the love of Jesus to the whole world, according to His command in Mark 16:15. Today, we still focus on youth, but we have members (known as "YWAMers") of almost every age and many of our short-term efforts have grown into long-term endeavours that have impacted lives and nations.

YWAM has a decentralized structure that encourages new vision and the exploration of new ways to change lives through training, convey the message of the gospel and care for those in need. We are currently operating in more than 1000 locations in over 180 countries, with a staff of over 18,000.

YWAM offers an introduction to missions called a Discipleship Training School or a DTS for short. These courses are excellent for testing the waters for missions and as an introduction to the ministry in general. The benefits of these courses will last a lifetime, even if you never go to the mission field.

They offer training and opportunities that will keep you with an extended support team during your missions training and group outreach. They also introduce you to community living in an operational environment and some overseas living. This ministry has over sixteen thousand full-time staff in over six hundred established bases worldwide. They also offer land-based outreaches everywhere in the world, and you will always be with a team, housed on a YWAM base in your host country. YWAM has a fleet of ships used for mercy ministries such as medical, food, and relief supplies, as well as ministry training for indigenous pastors.

http://www.ywam.org

5. Mercy Ships.

Mercy Ships is a global charity that has operated hospital ships in developing nations since 1978. Mercy Ships brings hope and healing to the forgotten poor by mobilizing people and resources worldwide, and serving all people without regard for race, gender, or religion. Large ocean going vessels provide hospital services and health care to the poor in port areas around the world. Volunteers help onboard the world's largest non-governmental hospital ship, the *Africa Mercy*. Both medical and non-medical positions are available.

The Mercy Ships Anchor Church program is a method for churches of any size to partner with Mercy Ships. There are many different levels depending on what best suits your church. Mercy Teams is your solution for short-term service opportunities. We have many opportunities, both long-term and short-term, in areas including health care, IT, administration, teaching, communications, stewards, and in deck and engineering.

They offer short and long term mercy ministry opportunities. Outreaches are all aboard ship, with travel adventures in various ports of call throughout the world. Mercy Ships missionaries are part of a shipboard team. This ministry has several fully functional hospital ships up to 515 feet long and a shorter ship of 250 feet in length. This is a good start for an introduction to community living and service. They are excellent organizations and your safety will be assured. They are on the web at http://www.mercyships.org/.

http://www.mercyships.org

6. Campus Crusade for Christ International (or Cru)

Campus Crusade for Christ or Cru (CCC) is committed to establishing spiritual movements everywhere so that everyone in the world knows someone who truly follows Jesus Christ. From college campuses to doctors, the United Nations to the inner city, we want to build spiritual movements. Helping to fulfill the Great Commission in the power of the Holy Spirit by winning people to faith in Jesus Christ, building them in their faith and sending them to win and build others; and helping the Body of Christ do evangelism and discipleship. Campus Crusade is looking for men and women who want to join what God is doing around the world.

I highly recommend the CCC mailing and database software called "tntMPD". Refer to the section "A word about Networking" for more information about this very helpful software.

> Campus Crusade for Christ International, or Cru
> 100 Lake Hart Drive
> Orlando, FL 32832
>
> Web Site: www.ccci.org
>
> 1-888-CRUSADE (1-888-278-7233)

7. International Mission Board (Southern Baptist Church)

A Southern Baptist Convention, IMB is supported by the Cooperative 'Lottie Moon Christmas Offering' and is a registered trademark of Woman's Missionary Union.

> http://www.imb.org

8. Gateway Missionary Training Center

This is an excellent missionary training center based in Canada. It is a unique missionary training community that focuses on equipping the whole person for service in another country.

Gateway Missionary Training Centre
21233-32 Avenue
Langley, BC V2Z 2E7
CANADA

Tel: 1-604-530-4283
Fax: 1-604-530-7192
email: info@gatewaytraining.org

http://www.gatewaytraining.org/contact.html

9. Chalmers Center

Chalmers Center also offers an e-mail-based distance learning course on the issues surrounding short-term missions (less than one month) in the context of the socio-economic poor. This course presents frameworks for considering the issues so that the benefits of mission projects are maximized and potential harm is minimized.

The training is appropriate for:
1) Sending churches and denominations
2) Host churches and missionaries
3) Mission project leaders
4) Mission team members

Cost of the three-week course was $55 (USD) plus the cost of separately ordered course material. Because the course is e-mail-based, slow dial-up speed will not limit participation. Furthermore, note that you may spend 6-8 hours per week on course work. To learn more, or to register, visit:

The Chalmers Center
Covenant College
14049 Scenic Highway
Lookout Mountain, GA, 30750, USA

1-706-956-4119
info@chalmers.org

http://www.chalmers.org

10. Brigada

Brigada is a wealth of resource information for those interested in short or long term missions. **Brigada** is a growing collection of web- and email-based resources staged from the offices of Team Expansion at Emerald Hills in Louisville, Kentucky, USA. *Brigada Today* a web journal offering resources, strategy tips, tools & "hacks" to Great Commission Christians. For a free subscription to the Brigada's weekly mission publication, visit Brigada on the web at www.brigada.org.

Brigada Editor
4112 Old Routt Road, Louisville, KY 40299 USA
Phone 1-502-719-0007

11. Constant Contact

This organization is a web-based newsletter creation and distribution system that costs about $150 a year for non-profit subscription. It's easy to set up and use, and it's very professional. Constant Contact®, Inc. helps small businesses, associations, and nonprofits connect with their customers, clients, and members. Constant Contact champions the needs of small organizations and provides them with an easy and affordable way to build successful, lasting customer relationships.

Constant Contact
Reservoir Place
1601 Trapelo Road

Waltham, MA 02451
Fax: 781-472-8101

www.ConstantContact.com
Phone 1-866-876-8464

12. People Raising

The People Raising website will lead you to a wealth of help in raising friends for your ministry and will help you build a solid base of support partners. It'll give your friend-raising team the help and tools they need to present a very well written newsletter. They provide conferences, DVDs or MP3s, study guides, spreadsheet software, and books to help you.

> www.PeopleRaising.com
> Email info@PeopleRaising.com
> Phone 847-971-6252
> People Raising offers:
> A People Raising book
> 6 Hour Training in DVD, CD, MP3
> Conferences, a newsletter, and tip of the month
> Bill Dillon, President

> Email: Bill@peopleraising.com

> Phone: 1-847-635-8902

13. RosettaStone

Rosetta Stone Inc. is a leading provider of technology-based language-learning solutions. Rosetta Stone Version 4 TOTALe is a complete solution that adds live conversational practice and social learning activities to our core course. Customers acquire language by discovering it naturally and intuitively, without translation or memorization. Speech Activation™ builds speaking confidence using state-of-the-art speech recognition technology while Native Socialization™ places customers in live interactive.

Available in more than 30 languages, RosettaStone language-learning solutions are used by schools, organizations and millions of individuals in over 150 countries throughout the world. The company is based in Arlington, Va.

For more information, visit RosettaStone.com.

> To contact RosettaStone call:
> Reilly Brennan
> rbrennan@RosettaStone.com
> 1-703-387-5863

14. Pimsleur Approach

Pimsleur approach is intended to attract those individuals and groups interested in achieving essential and cost-effective spoken language proficiencies. We have many languages to choose from including; Arabic, Chinese, and Japanese along with several others that quickly allow anyone to establish rapport and basic respect on trips abroad.

For comments or inquiries call us toll-free at (866)204-7139 and inquiries to CustomerCare@PimsleurApproach.com

> www.PimsleurApproach.com
> 1-866-204-7139

15. Wycliffe Bible Translators

About 340 million people do not have *any Scripture* in their language. Wycliffe's vision is to see the Bible accessible to all people in the language they understand best. To make this vision a reality, Wycliffe also focuses on community development, literacy development and church partnerships.

Wycliffe was founded in 1942 by William Cameron Townsend. A missionary to the Cakchiquel Indians of Guatemala, Townsend caught the vision for translation when Cakchiquel-speaking men expressed their concern that the Bible was not available to them in the language they understood clearly. As a result, Townsend resolved that every man, woman and child should be able to read God's Word in their own language.

Since its inception, Wycliffe has made great progress in Bible translation all around the world. To date, Wycliffe has played a part in completing more than 700 Scripture translations.

www.wycliffe.org

P.O. Box 628200
Orlando, FL 32862

Communication

If you have access to a computer I recommend using SKYPE. Skype is a computer to computer voice phone service with text and video conferencing available. Regular computer to computer calls with Skype are free. Two additional features are ON-Skype and Off-Skype for only pennies a minute for international phone calls. On-Skype allows you to call from your phone into the Skype network and Off-Skype allows you to call a phone off the network. With On-Skype and Off-Skype together, you can call from your local phone to another phone anywhere in the world for pennies a minute.

www.skype.com

Other mission agencies

For denominational mission boards, contact your local pastor or church office. There are quite a number of good mission agencies available. Contact as many agencies as you feel for a fair comparison, but ultimately seek the Lord for the right one. This venture will need to be bathed in prayer. Many will be okay to begin with, but as your experience and maturity grows, you will be able to bring one field into focus. This may take several months or several years, or a lifetime.

Mission agencies can be a good source of advice and help. They will give you a lot of help in evaluating your call or where you are in the process. Find the one that has a focus close to the call of your heart. They will not all be a match for you because we're not all alike and our callings are not all alike. God has a calling for you and for where you are at this point in your life.

Participating in short-term outreaches will help you feel comfortable with missions, until the field narrows to a people group, a location, and/or a ministry. You may find that a short-term mission with your denomination or local church ministry is your calling! The important point is not what you do or where you go, but to find the *right* ministry calling for you. All callings are valid and none should be of a lesser value. God's call on your life is His design, tailored just for you.

Focus your energy on your quest and nurture it. You may be surprised to see where the Lord takes you. However, you may not begin full-time, long-term missions until you are actually retired from a secular job and free to follow your heart's desire. Your preparation could be a lifetime, but you will be prepared and ready when the time comes for whatever God has for you. Until you are a mature missionary, and you speak the native language, do not go on your own or go alone. It is always best to go with a team or a partner you can pray with and rely on. Take this advice to the bank.

God will never call you to leave your responsibilities to someone else. If your responsibility is for your family, elderly parents, needy children, career needs, or even ministry preparation itself, the

Lord will not call you to leave them. He will call you when you're prepared, available, mature, and ready to go. It's in His time. You may not feel ready; in fact, you may never feel ready. But follow your heart and then go when the opportunity presents itself, and when you are free to go unhindered by life's needs. God is the master of circumstances. If the circumstances line up with your heart, and your prayer partners are in agreement, go for it.

If you are not completely free to go, or you have legal or moral responsibilities at home, do not go. God will not call you to leave a messy trail behind you as you leave, no matter how much enthusiasm and zeal you have. If you are in a tough situation, you can be a prayer partner for someone else until the time comes that you are free to go. Cultivate your energies to build a prayer team, a support team, and to raise concern for your field of interest. If you persist and go without God's blessing, it will be a disaster, and you will return home defeated and discouraged. Please don't do this to yourself. Wait for God's green light before you move.

Church outreaches

Gradually expand your horizon by participating in outreaches farther afield from your local church community. For example, begin with a church singles ministry, progress to a local rescue mission or a nursing home ministry, and share activities with other churches, cities, states, and finally the nations.

Consider all your outreach experiences not as an end to themselves but as training experiences for the calling God has for you. Every activity builds your experience and confidence on the previous activity, and you will gain personally from every outreach in which you participate.

When you're prepared and ready, wait!

Wait for the Lord to move first and then move into your ministry opportunity. The Lord's timing will be right, but if you try to move ahead of Him, you will be setting yourself up for trouble. If you move ahead of the Lord you may have to backtrack and start over again and retrace your steps! You will grow from the experiences of jump-starts and wrong directions, but I can assure you it will be costly. You'll learn to wait on the Lord and listen to that still small voice the hard way (like me.)

You may reach a point of frustration or even think you'll never move into your calling, but don't fear—God has not forgotten you, He knows where you live. As you will find later, there was a reason for a delay. Although you felt ready at the time, the Lord did not open the door for a reason. If you wait on the Lord, you will be very thankful. His delay perhaps saved you great loss to the point of even prolonging your life. Stay in prayer and wait for the Lord. When at all possible, confirm your major decisions with your support team. They are in partnership with you and may be seeing things from God's perspective more clearly than you.

Don't be a User

I knew of a person in a foreign country who called for help numbers of times, to a ministry I was working with. He came to our city on social visits but never once stopped in to say hello. He never once said thanks or communicated by phone or email except when he wanted something. He did not reciprocate help in any way even when it would have been easy for him and would have probably benefited him. Once he became known as a User, he received no further help from any of the ministries I was working with. He was essentially on his own. I understand he has since left the ministry and is working in a secular job in the foreign country. He lost a lot of good friends and rewards of those friendships.

Once you are in-country, you will need to develop a friendship network with your co-workers. If you continue to develop your friendship-based network, but only use your friends when you need them, you will become known as a "User." Other coworkers will begin to think the only reason you want their friendship is because they're useful to you, and you only call them when you need something. A User is someone who calls for help in a situation and never calls for any other reason. They don't help they are asked; they are always too busy or not available to help when help is needed. The User never says thank you or tries to visit when they come to town because they do not need anything from you anymore.

Once you become known to your associates as a "User," you will lose your friends and their willingness to come to your aid when you need it the most. Once you get this reputation, you will begin to be isolated from those who would be valuable allies. You will begin to be excluded from critical meetings, opportunities, and relationships. Your ministry will suffer long-term consequences, and this may be very subtle, but it will become more apparent as time goes on. You will become more isolated from your community of peers.

Your relationships in ministry and networking are good. However, guard your reasons for the relationship. Do not maintain a network for just contacting people when you need them. Be a friend first and your relationships and a team spirit will follow.

Journaling

A journal is a notebook of your personal writing. It's not a diary, but it is a place to record your experiences, reactions, and observations. You will be recording what you've done, heard, seen, read, or remembered. It's about people and places, faces, smells, and the human experience in your personal experience. You can include news clippings, sayings, snapshots—anything you would like to recall or consider in the future.

Keep a journal of your outreach experiences. At a later date these entries will be a priceless record of your experiences and will bring back many memories and help you learn from your own spiritual growth. Here are a few suggestions to consider as you record your experiences and feelings:

Points to consider in your journal:

1.) New friends you made and what made this friendship grow
2.) Surprises you found and what surprised you about yourself
3.) Spiritual truths you learned and what difference they make
4.) Mistakes you made and how you can avoid them next time
5.) Misunderstandings and how they could have been avoided
6.) Hardships that developed and how you dealt with them
7.) Conflicts that developed and why
8.) How the hardships or conflicts were resolved
9.) How you will deal with those hardships or conflicts next time
10.) What you would do differently if you could do this trip again
11.) How you can prepare for the next outreach
12.) What you discovered about yourself that you could do through Christ who strengthened you

God will use every outreach experience for your personal growth so when and where you go is not a life or death decision. What you do and how you do it is not as important as what you personally gain from the experience. It's not even what you accomplish for the Lord and, while that is important, the important thing is your growth in Christ as a person. Sometimes the undesirable outreach destinations will bring you the most surprising blessings and could possibly change your life.

I have gone on outreaches kicking and screaming and when it came time to leave, I didn't want to go back home! By the time I had to leave, I would have gladly given away my airline ticket to stay in Beijing, China—a place where I had no desire to go to in the first place. Don't shy away from an outreach just because you do not have a love for the people group or location. Your participation should fit in with the opportunity, but do not manipulate the circumstances to your desire because you may just manipulate yourself out of a blessing.

About Cultural Sensitivity

Culture and being sensitive to culture is one of the most important elements of ministry in a foreign country: It's all about relationships and adding value to the people. Sensitivity to the culture will mean the difference between success and failure in your ministry. You do not make friends and build relationships by offending people and it is only a matter of time before cultural insensitivity will offend someone. Once people have been offended, your ministry effectiveness will be diminished and possibly shut down all together. Then you may as well go home because the people will have closed their hearts to you and the message.

People can be severely hurt by certain cultural expressions. For instance, some expressions may be okay in your home culture but offensive in a foreign culture. Watch your cultural habits very carefully. Ask the indigenous people about a cultural expression before you use it. Never use a cultural expression in jest because it may come across as mocking the culture. Be sure to always affirm the indigenous people. Paul also understood the need for cultural sensitivity:

> *For though I am free from all men, I have made myself a servant to all, that I might win the more; and to the Jews I became as a Jew, that I might win Jews; to those who are under the law, as under the law, that I might win those who are under the law; to those who are without law, as without law (not being without law toward God, but under law toward Christ) that I might win those who are without law; to the weak I became as weak, that I*

might win the weak. I have become all things to all men
that I might by all means save some. Now this I do for
the gospel's sake, that I may be partaker of it with you.
—1 Corinthians 9:19-23 (NKJV)

This does not imply you should be a doormat, which could very well be perceived as weakness and would create a negative or spiritually harmful perception with the people you are trying to reach. It is important to learn the verbal and non-verbal language of the people. Many hand signals have meanings that can be funny and/or offensive in a culture. Fortunately, many people appreciative of a foreigner trying to learn their language and culture, and they are willing to forgive and understand.

Ask your contacts to correct your mistakes as soon as possible and accept their correction graciously. They are willing to help you and their correction is for your good. Smile a lot; this goes a long way in building relationships (unless smiling has a bad connotation in the culture). Actively listen when people speak to you and make eye contact, unless the culture does not permit direct eye contact. In some cultures, direct eye contact is reserved only for intimate relationships and is offensive outside of an intimate relationship. Be sensitive to the non-verbal cultural signs and traits.

In some cultures being blunt or direct is offensive. It brings shame on the person being confronted and causes a person to "lose face." In an honor-based culture such as in the Middle East or Far East, losing face is a powerful humiliation. In some cultures, the best way to confront someone, and the acceptable way, is to tell the person's coworker and that person will tell the person with whom you really want to communicate. This is often more acceptable and does not cause the person to lose face.

An innocent habit of whistling in public in many of the countries of the former Soviet Union, especially Russia and Ukraine is not good. During the soviet era, only pickpockets whistled in pubic. It was a signal between them. Therefore, if you whistle in public, you will notice people gradually moving away from you. If you have a habit of talking loudly in public, people will move away from you. Loud talk draws attention and the listening ear of the secret police or the former KGB.

In the Soviet era, government agents listened to what everyone said, so it became very dangerous to speak in public. The fear of betrayal has been ingrained in the people to this day. If you notice your friends becoming very quiet in public such as on a tram, trolley, or bus, you will know it is not because you forgot to brush your teeth this morning. Something is going on that you are not aware of, so take a hint! Be quiet until you can talk privately and find out what's going on. Be sensitive to non-verbal cues.

Another important, but negative, trait to remember is arrogance. No one likes an arrogant person, but many North Americans have an attitude or persona that is interpreted as arrogant in other cultures. Americans do not necessarily mean to be arrogant, but sometimes, in an effort toward direct and clear communication, habits and mannerisms like this can be interpreted as arrogant or offensive in other cultures.

Eastern European culture has established standards of privacy in public restaurants, which includes speaking softly, especially in this state of the former Soviet Union. Drawing attention to one's self or to your group is not wise, perhaps even dangerous and simply not done. The culture of privacy in a restaurant has become part of the post-Soviet dining experience to this day.

One time I was on a ministry trip in Eastern Europe with three friends. Two had very limited exposure outside of the United States, while a coworker and I had lived in Eastern European and the Middle East and were more familiar with the significance of the culture.in a social public setting. In the former Soviet Union which was a fear-based culture privacy was dominant. We were in a restaurant one evening when one of the other ministry leaders began quizzing my coworker in a way that probably would not have been kind even in our home culture, and certainly not here. He was loud, accusative, demonstrative, and confrontational during the meal. This drew a lot of attention from other diners in the restaurant. Even the waiter drew away from us to the other end of the room. I felt very uncomfortable and wanted to walk outside but I was on the inside of the table against the wall. I could not remove myself from the table. I felt very bad for my coworker.

Other diners near us noticed the discussion and gave the appearance of being uncomfortable with us. I recognized their looks in our direction and this made me more uncomfortable. My friend handled it much better than I would have. He was in a position to shut down the conversation, but instead, let it go to the end. I felt bad for the ministry leader and wondered how many other offenses would be created before they became aware of cultural respect for other people in a foreign country. Irreparable damage can be done to a ministry by being insensitive to people of other cultures and offending those you are in ministry for. Respect for the culture is respect for the person.

Once a wall of offense has been established, it is difficult, if not impossible, to repair or reestablish favor. Fortunately, my coworker understood the ministry leader and his lack of understanding of the cultural environment. Their relationship survived this experience, but had my friend been with a person of the Eastern European culture we were in, the relationship would have been irreparably damaged. My friend's cultural understanding and ministerial maturity prevailed. Again, cultural sensitivity can make a ministry and cultural insensitivity can break a ministry. Unsurprisingly, the person causing the situation had caused offense in prior relationships in this country.

Whose culture is important here? Is it yours or theirs? Who is important here, you or them? Relationships are the bedrock of Christian ministry. Success in a foreign country is very dependent on your understanding of their language and culture; these two elements are the two legs of a three-legged relationship. The Gospel is the third leg of the relationship. God wants a relationship with Man and has ordained the Believer in Jesus to reach our fellow man with this message of salvation in Christ. These are men and women reaching men and women with the life saving message of salvation in Jesus Christ and a restored relationship with God.

Many cultures exist today because of human history and corporate relationships that have developed into nations. To go from one culture to another often requires *at least* a change in geography, language, economy, dress, and climate.

The ministry of missions is leaving our home culture to go to another culture, to take this universal message of salvation to another people group. One must embrace the new culture and language to reach the people in their culture and in their language. This does not mean converting the people to your culture—because that is not the goal. The goal is to take the message of the Gospel to a foreign culture, in the language of the people, without changing the meaning of the message.

Growth of the indigenous church body is a measure of our success or failure in sharing the Good News with our fellow man. The message must be taken to the new culture, in the language of the people so they understand the message. We are the fruit that bears the seed of the Gospel. The message is the seed and we are the carriers of the seed. It is the seed that is important, not the messenger. It's not our culture and it's not our way of life that is important. We have to relate the message through the native culture because it is the message that matters most.

My friend related this true event to me: A missionary couple from a western nation had been building a relationship with a local indigenous family and came to visit them and congratulate them on the arrival of their new baby. In that culture it is customary to present and open the gifts right away, so the missionary couple got their carefully wrapped gift out and presented it to the couple with the baby. The local mother gasped when she opened the gift! She was so shocked she started weeping and ran out of the room! Confused and ashamed, the Western couple just left the house.

Later, with the help of the local interpreter, they tried to understand what happened when the woman opened the gift. The interpreter asked them how the gift was wrapped. When she was told they had wrapped it in white paper, her eyes got big. They also told her they had included a card with a stork carrying a baby attached to the gift. The interpreter was completely horrified!

She said, "White is the color of death in our culture, so you wished these new parents that their baby would die! And the stork is a symbol of a scavenger on its way to take the dead body of their baby!"

The sad result of this cultural nightmare is that the relationship with this family was *never* restored, despite apologies and attempts at reconciliation. Think of the Gospel message of God's love as the most precious gift we would like to give to everyone around us and to the nations. How many times do we present it with our own cultural wrapping paper? When people say *no* to us, are they really saying no to God or could it be that the package offends them and the gift never gets opened?

Short-term outreach

Living in a foreign culture can be stressful, especially if we're not called to that culture. If you are indeed called to a people group, develop a sense of personal ownership of that culture and people. If you're not able to establish ownership in the people group, you will not be able to sustain a presence there. Your attitude and stress level is a measurement of your adaptation to the new culture. This is measurable. Your coworkers and the indigenous people will be able to see this even before *you* are able to recognize it.

Look for feedback from your coworkers and be sensitive to their reactions to you. Be honest and open with your native or foreign coworkers for the freedom to tell you when they sense problems in your personal and ministry life. They will give you clues to your success with the people and help your adjustment and assimilation into their community. Healthy friendships produce healthy long-term relationships.

I recommend some Rest & Recharge every three months or at least every six months at the most. You need to have your spiritual batteries recharged to keep you from experiencing burnout. Learn to pace yourself. Your stress level will be a barometer to tell you when to schedule some R&R. Don't wait until you are in trouble. The ministry will go on without you, and if it doesn't, maybe you need to back off and regroup.

God does not need a casualty on the mission field, so learn to guard your health and your well-being—mentally, physically, emotionally, and spiritually. God does not call you to sacrifice yourself or your family to serve Him, Jesus has already done this for you. Commit the ministry to God and let Him be responsible for it.

What not to do

When you are in a foreign land, it's important to ask for help from a prospective colleague or indigenous coworker as soon as possible. Find favor with the people before you try to minister to them or bring them the message. Develop a friendship or trust relationship with someone you feel is interested in the ministry and build a relationship in the right direction.

Friendship evangelism will build trust and relationship, and earn you the right to share the truth. Honor and respect the people and their culture. Humility and thoughtfulness opens many doors that would otherwise be closed to you. When people perceive you as a friend, you will be welcomed. This is important to them and since it's important to them, it's important to you. Honor them and they will honor you. Respect people and they will respect you. Help them and they will help you. Add value to them and they will open doors for a ministry. Pastor Bob Zuhl told me to always affirm people, and I have found that in affirming others, it came back to me many times over. Find those things that are affirming and expand on them.

On the other side of the coin, make it a point to find those things that are offensive and avoid them at all costs, even in jest. In many countries, the people have been downtrodden for so many years that they have a poor national or personal self-image and a haughty, insensitive spirit will reinforce that image. Do

AN ADVENTURE IN MISSIONS

not make fun of their toilets, their food or food service, their cars; nothing. Remember, it is the best they have, and you have no right to denigrate it. You have not earned that right. You will not make friends with a superior attitude, but humility will open doors to genuine friendships.

Do not behave like you would in your home culture—you are not in your home culture. People may not appreciate your home culture, as wonderful as it is, and will not understand it any more than you understand their culture. You are on someone else's turf now and their rules apply. It behooves you to learn the culture and language of the people you are called to serve and not expect them to learn your culture and language. Your goal is to bring the message of the Gospel to this people group at their level and in words they understand.

All your efforts to learn their language and culture will give you immense favor with the people you are called to reach. Do not force them to come to you. Reach out to them even when you do not think they respond the way you think they should. The Holy Spirit may be doing something in their hearts that you cannot perceive.

Don't draw attention to yourself. It is not about you or your ego. Watch the people and how they act in public or in private, at mealtime, or in public transportation. Do not make fun of their public facilities, even if they seem funny to you. After all, their public facilities are not funny to them and your humor could shame or insult them. Many cultures are shame-based or honor-based, and a joke told for a cheap laugh can have negative, long-range effects on your ministry. They may not say anything to you, and they may even laugh with you, but you can be sure they will remember even the slightest offense or putdown of their culture. You are a guest in their country, so respect that, and show respect to the people. The measure you give out will come back to you many times over.

Relationships

It's all about the relationships. Ministry is all about people and relationships. Most decisions are made strictly out of relationships, good or bad. Returning to the mission field after an absence, I went to work with my old friend Stewart Lieberman because of our relationship in ministry over the years. The Lord brings people together with complimentary gifting to form trust, and these relationships are built over time.

Very few of us are called to be a team of one. This may be necessary in a pioneering frontier-mission venture, but it is not wise for the long-term. Everyone in missions needs prayer partners on their team for accountability, to cover each other in protective prayer, and to do spiritual warfare on their behalf. Relationships and commitment to a relationship will hold ministries together when the attacks come. Do not think you can maintain yourself in ministry as a Lone Ranger.

Gifting and Talents

God has given you talents and gifts to match your calling. All you have to do is develop your gifts and talents to grow in Christ. Do not try to develop or use gifts you do not have. Do not try to copy someone else's gifts or talents. Be yourself, and be the person God created you to be. He created you for a reason and for a purpose, the way you are, warts and all. As you grow, you may be given new gifts and talents you had not seen—or simply did not have—before. This is growth, personal and spiritual. I recommend a book titled "Twelve Ordinary Men," by John MacArthur. You'll be encouraged by this.

Adding value to people

Show respect and honor, develop friendships, build trust and bond with the people, and you will find you are in covenant relationship with the people you are called to, and they are in covenant relationship with you.

AN ADVENTURE IN MISSIONS

Covenant-based relationships build value and effectiveness in a ministry. When you transition to a foreign people group, bridge the language barrier, and embrace their culture, you raise the value level of the people. This will be received with welcome. People see you "coming alongside" to help them. A covenant relationship will last through the good times and the bad times, and even after you are gone. That is when you know you've done your work well.

The call to a people group should be at no cost to the people group. Our salvation was provided to us at no cost, but it was costly none-the-less. Most people groups cannot afford to pay for your ministry, and that's not the way God intended it to be anyway. Salvation is free to the receiver. Attaching a price tag on ministry is not from the Lord and is looked on as a perversion in scripture.

It is a mistake to pour money into a people group by hiring administrative or ministry staff, and purchasing plant facilities with foreign money in the early stages. The indigenous ministry can be started this way, but it is generally not healthy for long-term growth. It is okay to hire interpreters and basic administrative staff, but plan to develop and grow your staff with the ministry. This will allow a time for your ministry and staff to bond together. It will also give you time to weed out those who want a nice salary from those who are genuinely seeking to minister to those in need and meet the needs of the ministry. Money may attract people to the ministry with the wrong motives. The Lord will bring the right people to your ministry as the ministry develops.

Money-based growth seems to block the spiritual growth of the people. I have seen ministries pour hundreds of thousands of US dollars into plant facilities, remodeling, and staff, and when they were done they had to shut it down because they only had a few indigenous people involved, no money left, and no ministry. Not only did they do this once but twice! They used the same model, and it failed both times. I've seen it on three occasions and with the same results!

But a certain man named Ananias, with Sapphira his wife, sold a possession. And he kept back part of the proceeds, his wife also being aware of it, and brought a certain part and laid it at the apostles' feet. But Peter said, "Ananias, why has Satan filled your heart to lie to the Holy Spirit and keep back part of the price of the land for yourself? While it remained, was it not your own? And after it was sold, was it not in your own control? Why have you conceived this thing in your heart? You have not lied to men but to God." Then Ananias, hearing these words, fell down and breathed his last. Great fear came upon all those who heard these things.—Acts 5:1-5 (NKJV)

Money is power and attracts people, in or out of a ministry. Money may attract people who see a ministry as another way to make a living. If you start the ministry by funding everything with foreign resources, you may wind up supporting it forever. The people will be forever dependent on your foreign support and will not grow spiritually enough to develop their own ministry support base. If you want to impress the folks back home, and build your support level, then get a building and send pictures. If you want to develop a self-sustaining indigenous ministry, develop the people and take pictures of *them* for the folks back home. These applications are not mutually exclusive, but people who pray and support you want to see pictures of people and lives changed for Christ.

Invest in people and not in plant facilities. Work on growing the people in ministry and allow them to have ownership of it. This will take longer, but the congregation that develops will be self-supporting, mature, and in time, able to send out missionaries without your support. They will become autonomous and self-supporting. As the congregation grows and matures, they will find a plant facility that's suitable to them and their culture. The Lord is growing His church, so He will manage the growth of the body. Your job is to be there for the people and assist in the growth process.

It is much better for a healthy long-term ministry to develop support from within the people group and the culture itself. Nurture ministry growth, and give the people ownership of the ministry from the beginning or as soon as possible. You will build a lasting and healthy ministry by investing in the people. It's okay to start small and build slowly, one by one. Do not worry about a small beginning. The important measure is the quality of the ministry, not the building, the size of the ministry, or the favor you have built with the local authorities, as important as that is.

An example of what not to do might be to build a western style church structure in a rural farming community where the people live in adobe structures with no electricity. They are used to living here and you are not. Do not build something that they are not used to. Adapt to the indigenous culture and lifestyle of the people you are trying to reach. Help them build an adobe shelter that the people are comfortable with and proud to own. Give them ownership of the ministry, and you will have done your job successfully.

Sage Wisdom

7

The following is a short list of combined wisdom:

1) Where He leads, He also provides. If your provisions are being met, you can pretty much assume He's leading. If they're not being met then you need to find out why—and if perhaps the Lord is leading you in another direction. The Lord may want you to trust Him and have faith in Him to provide for your needs. Maybe you are relying on your own strength when He wants you to rely on Him. Perhaps the enemy is coming against you. Consult with your prayer support team.

2) If He calls, you will have a confidence and know it. Persist in your calling even against seemingly closed doors, stand firm until you know which direction to go. Wait on the Holy Spirit to lead your way. He can open any door.

3) Have a group of intercessors in place on your team who are encouragers and prayer partners.

4) Maintain relationships at home and where you are.

5) Learn the language to understand the culture.

6) Avoid walking in the mentality of your home country.

7) In any foreign culture, it takes much longer to do things. If it took an hour at home, it will take you a day in the field. If it took a day at home, it will take you up to a week in the new culture—unless you get a native to do it for you.

8) Ask God to give you a heart of love for the people He's called you to. You will need this every day!

9) Things to do: Go to conferences, pray a lot, seek the "Where and How" of missions. Research on the internet for a people group that is on your heart. Develop occupational skills to aid your ministry search that may be useful in the new country.

10) Go on a short-term mission trip anywhere for the cross-cultural ministries experience and training. If possible, go to the selected people group or geographic location you are interested in. Read books about missions and missionaries. A biography "Is that You God?" by Loren Cunningham is a good start. Submit to your church or spiritual authority and ask God to give you a view of the world from His perspective

11) Last of all: your experience in missions will be unique to you and your time. Your experience will follow a pattern, but it won't be a duplicate of anyone else's experiences. This book is a help to reveal what others have experienced in God's call on their life. Your experiences will add to the sum of all experiences here.

12) Expect the unexpected. Remember the Law of Unintended Consequences: What you don't plan for will probably happen.

13) If you are in ministry and fall in love with someone who is not in ministry, there is a possibly you may wind up leaving the ministry. These things happen. It would be better to restrict any potential romantic relationships to someone who is active in ministry with a calling that matches yours. Act in haste, and you will repent in leisure.

Questions for Your Heart

This is not a pass/fail test. These questions are meant to be thought provoking and focus your thoughts in the right direction. They will help make the way clearer for you. If you are considering the mission field, these questions help you see the possibilities and how the mission field will affect you in the future.

This is not a litmus test for missions. Some people are called to full-time or long-term missions; some calls are for part-time or short-term missions; some calls are for a season; and some people are called to pray and support missions. Your calling has been designed by God to fit the unique you and to fulfill God's call on your life. He designed it just for you and you for it!

The key is to identify your calling and then go for it. This is your opportunity to serve the King of Kings and to be involved in the most exciting adventure of your life. Ponder these questions and keep a journal as you track your progress. Some questions may have little meaning to you and some may jump off the page for you. Be sensitive to patterns that will reveal your direction. Record your thoughts and answers to your prayers in your journal. This will clarify your direction and show you how the Lord is directing your life.

Here are a few thoughts to add to your journal as you consider your call:

1) Why are you interested in missions?
2) Do you have a heart for people or a specific people group?
3) Do you have a heart to serve wherever you're asked?

4) Do you have a specific ministry focus?
5) What is your timeline of availability?
   a. Is the desire there, but the timing's not right?
   b. Is the call for a future date?
   c. Is the present time right?

6) Do you have an adventurous spirit?
7) Do you enjoy experiencing other cultures?
8) Are you willing to leave home to serve the Lord?
9) Does living in a foreign land sound attractive?
10) Can you work alone and unsupervised?
11) Is anything holding you back? God will not call you to sacrifice your family or other responsibilities even if He has a call to missions on your heart or your life. Some responsibilities that might delay your participation in outreaches include:
   a. What are your family responsibilities?
   b. What are your economic responsibilities?
   c. What are your needs for specific ministry training and preparation?
   d. Are you adequately prepared?
   e. Does your pastor or elder feel you are not yet prepared?

12) Do you put a higher value on people than possessions?
13) Do you run from difficult times or endure them?
14) Are you willing to begin training now for future ministry?
15) What are you doing now?
16) Are you being faithful in the small things?
17) Are you serving now and in submission to authority?
18) How much time do you think would be reasonable to invest in pre-field training: Three months, six months, or a year?
19) How interested would you be in enrolling in a pre-field training program that offered a combination of live teaching and distance education?

20) Would you be interested in enrolling in a program of study that offered in-service and/or on-the-job training to help you adjust and become effective on the field?

21) What values would you look for in missionary training?

    a. Mentoring, discipleship, and coaching by an experienced missionary?

    b. Lectures and course work?

    c. Living in a meaningful missionary community?

    d. Modeled and participative learning?

    e. Cross-cultural and multi-cultural exposure?

    f. Language skills?

    g. Evangelization skills and techniques development?

    h. Interpersonal relationship skills development?

    i. Spiritual warfare training?

    j. Church planting skills and techniques?

    k. Worldview and world mission perspectives?

    l. Ministering to children?

    m. Relief and economic development?

    n. Fund-raising and developing prayer partners?

Forwarding Agents

Do You Need A Forwarding Agent?

Thanks to Jason Casey for taking time to assemble these "Top 10" lists regarding forwarding agents—those unsung heroes that take care of missionaries who serve cross-culturally. Jason is a missionary serving with Team Expansion in Europe.

A forwarding agent handles all your records and accounts back home. They send newsletters, pay bills, forward your mail, and make sure your insurance and social security are covered and your financial support is in the account when you need it. Most get 5% of your support income and some get as high as 10% for their services, unless this service is their personal missionary service and calling. I know of one sending agency that gets 17%, but they also provide extended services like a laptop computer, R&R expense coverage, and other such expenses. If they are good, they are worth every penny for the peace of mind.

Most sending agencies provide a full or partial forwarding agency service as a part of their administrative service for people in their organization. I recommend a personal forwarding agent, who is a member of your support team. You have a personal relationship with a support team member, and they have a backup in the event of over-riding schedule. The burden is not on one or two people, but on a team of people. If it's on one or two people, the responsibility can be stressful, and it could mean the loss of your support services on occasion.

Top 10 ways you know you have a _good_ forwarding agent:

10. They identify with the missionaries' call to that particular people, country and ministry
9. They are willing to travel to learn and represent the ministry
8. They remind the family of the need for more photos or more "field stories" to be included in communiqués to supporters
7. They balance the books in a timely fashion
6. They pray for fruit from your efforts
5. They make some of the mission arrangements for furlough
4. They have a servant's heart
3. They are a husband and wife forwarding agent ministry
2. Plain and simple: Their strong point is accuracy
1. They have basic computer know-how

Top 10 reasons you _don't need_ a forwarding agent:

10. Missionaries never need urgent, middle-of-the-night bank transfers
9. Missionaries love to stuff and address two hundred envelopes every month
8. Missionaries can handle their own finances, thank you very much
7. Missionaries always receive their mail overseas intact and quickly
6. It is cheap, quick, and easy to mail things from overseas
5. It is easy to cash out-of-country personal checks overseas
4. Foreign banks are safe, convenient, and reliable
3. It is easy to call American 800 phone numbers from overseas
2. Ah, who needs accountability anyway?
1. IRS . . . what does that stand for again?

Top 10 signs you need a _new_ forwarding agent:

10. You get a copy of your newsletter printed on a piece of newspaper
9. You go to file a claim with your health insurance company only to find out your policy has been canceled by your forwarding agent "to cut down on expenses"
8. When you turn 65, you find out your IRA payments have been mailed into the NRA instead and your forwarding agent is a member of the NRA
7. Your forwarding agent raised his commission to 10% of your support
6. You see your forwarding agent picketing on TV during a news story covering a forwarding agent strike demanding more benefits
5. When you ask them to run a financial report, they ask, "How do I turn the computer on again?"
4. On their way to your mission agency's "Forwarding Agent Training" they decided to stop at Six Flags instead
3. When you call to chat, one of their children answers the phone and you hear them angrily say, "Dad, it's that missionary guy again that's always asking you to run errands and do favors or offer support!"
2. You read in the church bulletin that your current forwarding agent just got out of the hospital after having outpatient, prosthetic finger replacement surgery from all the paper cuts from stuffing envelopes year after year
1. One day out of the blue you hear from them "we've decided to be missionaries"

Mission Categories

Comparison of Culture and Language

Type 1: *Common Culture / Common Language*

When a missionary and his mission field share a common culture and common language this could be referred to as a "Home Missions" ministry. It would include an Inner-city outreach, a rescue mission ministry, or a neighborhood children's ministry. Everyone may live in the same city, neighborhood, or possibly be as far away as another state or region of the country, but the common bonds are culture and language.

Type 2: *Common Culture / Different Language*

When a missionary shares a common culture, but speaks a different language, there are probably crossing ethnic boundaries yet remaining on a common ground of culture and/or nationality. The shared culture is the common bond. This is more common in large metropolitan areas or geographic areas with an immigrant population.

An example might be a local San Diego church outreach into the Latino Barrio of San Diego or Tijuana, Mexico. We share a culture but our native language is different.

Type 3: *Different Culture / Common Language*

When the missionary has different cultural values, but shares a common language, he or she still has a common ground of language to work on. A ministry under these circumstances is not difficult, but care must be taken to affirm the other culture. This could be characterized as an urban ministry outreach to an inner city neighborhood.

An example might be a church in Philadelphia, Pennsylvania sending an outreach team to London, England. We speak the same language, but the culture is different. Cultural sensitivity is important.

Type 4: *Different Culture / Different Language*

When people have a different culture and a different language, the barriers must be looked at as a whole. By immersing in a new culture, a missionary can quickly learn to embrace the new society. And when language and culture are learned together, the learning process accelerates.

Knowledge of God's call on your life ahead of time and your preparation can ease the transition into the new culture and environment. The language can be learned before you arrive at your destination, but the language and cultural awareness will be perfected or more complete when you are in country. An example might be an American outreach to Ukraine where the language transition is from English to Ukrainian or Russian, and the cultural shift is from a Western culture to an Eastern culture. All the preparation in the world will not match the experiences and learning you gain on the ground in your new home. However, preparation helps immensely.

It is hard to predict how adjustments to the new country will work out for you. It may be a rapid transition, or it may take considerable time for you to feel comfortable in the new culture. Language transition may take several years for you to become fluent, and in many cases, and you will never reach the level of, say, writing poetry like a native speaker. Don't worry; it probably won't hamper your ministry's effectiveness. In fact, may increase it. It will create an interest in the people to learn your language.

The difference between a Western culture and mind-set and an Eastern culture and mind-set is vast. A Western culture and mind-set emphasizes the truth being more important than the relationship. Those in the west value independent thinking and individual decision-making. They are encouraged to think outside the box and to challenge the status quo.

An Eastern culture and mind-set emphasizes the relationship being more important than the truth. They value thinking inside the box with no independent decision-making outside the box. A Muslim can know that Jesus is the way, the truth, and the life and must believe in Him for salvation, and yet turn his back on this because the family is Muslim. To become a believer in Jesus is to break tradition and dishonor their family and their country. To dishonor their family and their country can be a death sentence.

Since most Islamic countries are religious and operate under Sharia law, to become a Christian is to deny Islam, dishonor your country, and bring great shame on the family. Sometimes the family will be severely persecuted because a member of the family has become a Christian. The only way to avoid this shame and dishonor is to kill the offending family member.

In addition, to become a suicide bomber will gain great honor for the family and bring a reward for them in the form of employment security, community recognition, and a lump sum cash payment to the family. An honor/shame-based culture is reinforced with money, religious approval, and societal acceptance.

Comparison of General and Specific Ministries Definitions

There are two basic types of missionary service: *General* and *specific*.

A **Generalist** is equipped for a variety of ministry-related tasks yet not specializing in any one. They're kind of a jack-of-all-trades in the ministry, which is the norm of mission's service. On the other side, a **specialist** is one called to meet a single ministry need or is one who has a single overriding specialty skill. An example might be a crusade evangelist: They hit and run, like a birthing team, and then leave the growth of the new believers to a pastor and generalist for nurturing follow up.

Sometimes formal training and specialization in a particular segment of the ministry can be a disadvantage in the mission field or in a foreign culture. A generalist such as a pastor is needed to lead a ministry and cover all the ministry needs of the congregation. But a specialist, such as a street evangelist or church planter, is needed to face specific needs of the ministry. Change is a basic part of the ministry and multitasking is the norm. As an analogy, a generalist is like a soldier on the ground that does the every day ministry development and stays with the church. The specialist is the paratrooper who drops in to perform a needed specialty and leaves after it's done.

Often there are not enough people available in the work of the ministry to afford the luxury of specialization. Cultural circumstances and congregation needs must direct the ministry and not the specialization. While training and a specialty are good, flexibility and a servant heart are most important.

The *general categories* are those with broadly defined or undefined categories in ministry, location, or people groups. People in this category are available to serve where needed most. They tend to be a generalist, one whose ministry is defined by the need, the people they work with, or where they go.

An example of someone in this general category would be a volunteer with a mission agency, doing what is needed to help the ministry with any people group, or in any country. On an outreach in May, they might be painting (ministry) in a mission station in La Cruz, Mexico (location and people group), and in another outreach three months later, they might be cooking (ministry) for an inner city outreach (people group) in Hoboken, New Jersey (location).

The *specific category* is with clearly defined ministry, location, or people group. A specific grouping would be the distinguishing factor of identification.

An example of a specific identification would be a specific ministry, to a specific people, at a specific location such as teaching English as a Second Language (defined ministry), in San Diego, California (specific location), for Mexican immigrants (identifiable people group). Another category, Mobile or Stationary, is also included in the following table. The table helps illustrate the three mission focus categories: Ministry, Location, and People Group. These categories, combined with a General and/or Specific nature, will help you identify where you might best fit in a foreign culture setting.

General Ministry

A person called to a general ministry does not have a narrowly defined ministry focus but can function in multiple areas of need. They may be able to act as a cook, counselor, evangelist, gardener, translator, or carpenter with equal ease, and they are not limited to any one area specialty. Some ministry skills require professional-level training and expertise, and it is possible this person may not function at that level, but they can function well enough for the task at hand.

An example might be a retired person with several levels of life skills that allow him or her to function in overlapping areas of need. Another example might be a young person who can fill general needs because they are willing and able to adapt and learn quickly.

Specific Ministry

A person with a specific ministry skill could be referred to as a specialist, one called and trained for specialized areas of the ministry. The focus is on areas such as evangelism, finance and accounting, administration, translation, or grounds maintenance, etc. They often tend to support or build on the work of others, such as a person with a general calling who has cleared the path or laid a foundation for them to build on. They work to support an established congregation with the special ministry to meet the needs in the body of Christ.

An example might be a person who ministers in discipleship and counseling at a local church ministry or regionally in discipleship and counseling training for multiple churches. The ministry is the focus and defining element of his or her calling.

General Location

A general location refers to an undefined, unlimited, or unrestricted geographic or geopolitical area of the ministry. Location certainly isn't the defining element of the ministry. In fact, location actually makes little difference to the ministry as it spans locations. This span has a base ministry with a short-term application in any specific location. People with this calling adapt quickly.

An example might be a person with a specialized teaching ministry that takes them from teaching for a week in Equatorial Africa and the next week in Oslo, Norway. They will feel at home and function with equal ease in either location because the defining element is not the location but the ministry.

Specific Location

This is a ministry restricted to a specific location such as a defined geographic or geopolitical boundary. It could be a village, town, city, or province, home group, or organized church. Those with general and specific ministry specialties are called to fill the needs and responsibilities at this location, in every segment of the ministry, to build the Body of Christ.

An example would be one called to Belfast, Ireland, but not outside of Belfast. They support the cross-cultural ministry needs, staying focused on the Belfast area. Ministry will depend on the needs of the area such as pastor, teacher, counselor, carpenter, church planter, cook, or helper for example.

General People Group

This refers to an undefined, unlimited, or unrestricted focus on an identifiable people group. The ministry focus is on all people in a geographic, geopolitical, or culture field with no preferences.

A good agency example is YWAM (Youth With A Mission.) This mission organization takes outreaches to every country in the world, all the time! These emissaries on outreach seek to minister to people groups cross culturally, no matter the diversification of people in the area. They go to different people groups on every outreach: to India, Holland, Africa, South America, China, and to the ends of the earth and are inclusive of all people groupings. There are well over thirteen thousand full-time people with YWAM, worldwide.

Specific People Group

A call to a specific people group refers to those called to minister to a targeted people group to the exclusion of other groups, perhaps even in the same area. The Generalist will have a broad spectrum of ministry skills to meet the needs of the people. Specialists will be called to provide ministry training for the church body such as evangelism, pastoral care, church planters, music and worship leaders, discipleship leaders, etc. Some specialists may be called for language and cross-cultural training for the building up of the Body of Christ.

An example of a specialist might be one called to minister to the Druze of Northern Israel, but will not have a ministry focus with any other people group in Northern Israel. Their ministry people grouping may also include the Druze in Turkey as they are in the same people group but living in different geographic and geopolitical area.

Mobile or Stationary

Those called to a mobile ministry are like a roving seed planter. They're always on the move. Something like Johnny Appleseed who planted apple seeds wherever he went. Short-term, church-based outreaches and organizations can fall into this category. They go on outreach to different countries, locations, or people groups on every outreach.

They're breaking ground for those who follow with a specific call on their lives to minister in those specific locations or people groups. Those with a call to a specific location or people group are the stationary follow-up to the mobile seed planter. They could be likened to those special soldiers who advance behind enemy lines ahead of the Army, to prepare the way.

A Matrix of Ministry Types

Type	Ministry	Location	People group
1.	General	General	General
2.	General	General	Specific
3.	General	Specific	General
4.	General	Specific	Specific
5.	Specific	General	General
6.	Specific	General	Specific
7.	Specific	Specific	General
8.	Specific	Specific	Specific
9.	Mobile or Stationary		

General and Specific Examples

Type 1. General Ministry / General Location / General People Group

One who is called to short-term outreaches or who goes with a variety of agencies or churches to different geographic locations. This person doesn't go with a specific ministry calling, but their individual tasks vary with the needs of the outreach.

Type 2. General Ministry / General Location / Specific People Group

One who is called to a specific people group might be characterized by a short-term outreach or a long-term mission call to a targeted people or language group. Ministry occurs in various cities, regions, and countries but always to an exclusive, identifiable segment of the people.

An example might be an outreach to a particular tribe of Indian peoples who live in several countries or regions in Central America. Another example would be a calling to the Navajo Native Americans in the Southwest United States, who live in different states but belong to the same tribal peoples.

Type 3. General Ministry / Specific Location / General People Group

This is a ministry that would include all peoples in a specific location such as a city or country town.

An example of one called to a specific location might be ministering with all peoples in Istanbul, Turkey such as Muslims, Christians, Jews, and Kurds whose ethnic identity is different, yet they share a national identity and a common language. The ministry will be to meet the needs as they present themselves. This person could be a church planter, evangelist, or a discipleship ministry.

Type 4. General Ministry / Specific Location / Specific People Group

A person called to minister at a specific location and to a specific people group may exercise a broad spectrum of ministry skills within these boundaries. This is an exclusive ministry to the people and to the location.

An example might be a call to work with the Jewish people in Tel Aviv or the Palestinian people in Tel Aviv, but not both people groups in Tel Aviv. Even though these two people groups live in the same city, there's a language and cultural separation between them that requires specific ministry focus.

Type 5. Specific Ministry / General Location / General People Group

A specific ministry to a general or non-specific location and general or non-specific people group is a Ministry Specialist, meeting special ministry needs among the body of Christ at multiple locations.

An example might be a someone who travels to different locations training people in healing ministries, music and worship, pastoral care, evangelism, church planting, medical ministries, or discipleship.

Type 6. Specific Ministry / General Location / Specific People Group

A ministry specialist, called to a specific people group, but without a defined location or boundary, is similar to Type 2 with the difference of having a ministry specialty to the special people group.

An example of this calling might be a traveling evangelist among the Ogallala Sioux Native Americans of the North and South Dakota. State boundaries do not define their identity as a people group. Another example might be one called to lead a home group ministry among the Cuban people of metropolitan Miami, Florida, and New Orleans, Louisiana.

Type 7. Specific Ministry / Specific Location / General People Group

A ministry specialist, called to a specific location, to minister to all people at that location.

An example of this might be one called to pastor a church, or be a ministry leader at First Wesleyan Church in Battle Creek, Michigan, where location and ministry are the defining elements.

Another example would be one called to pastor a church that cares for both Jews and Arabs in the same congregation, such as Adonai Roi Messianic Congregation in Tel Aviv, Israel.

Type 8. Specific Ministry / Specific Location / Specific People Group

A ministry specialist called to a specific location and to a specific people group is tightly focused. The ministry specialty, location, and people group may change over time, which will change this category.

An example might be teaching the fifth grade boys (specific people group) Sunday school class (a ministry specialty) at First Baptist Church of Powder Springs, Georgia (a specific location). This person should be under pastoral or board supervision and leadership oversight for accountability. In this setting, they would fit this category of specific ministry, specific location, and specific people group.

Another example might be a prison chaplain (general ministry) with a focus on discipleship and counseling (specific ministry). The church family is centered on the prisoners (specific people group) in one location (sort of a captive audience!).

Type 9. Mobile or Stationary

There are two additional categories of Mobile and Stationary that helps to clarify ministry.

A. **Mobile Ministries**

A mobile missionary or ministry would be ministering in different locations, such as the circuit riders of the old west. They would pastor several churches for the same or different denominations because of the absence of available pastors. They would hold services in the morning in one town and another town in the evening. This exists today in rural areas of many countries of the world because of the absence of qualified pastors in the areas.

Many underground congregations in restricted access countries have pastors who fit this category. These mobile pastors support a network of underground small groups in the Body of Christ. They meet in homes or even caves or in private shelters to shield them from neighbors who are hostile to the Gospel. Some house churches play secular music on the radio outside of the meeting place so those outside will not hear praise and worship on the inside.

Other missionaries make monthly trips across borders to bring teaching aides and training materials to indigenous churches that are usually rural and that have limited funds for ministry growth. The missionaries in this category have an ongoing ministry with a specific location or people group, but do not reside in the area they are called to minister in. They need mobility to be able to supply the people with teaching and materials for healthy church growth.

B. <u>**Stationary Ministries**</u>

A stationary pastor or missionary category is more common. They remain with one congregation, in one town or city, but with perhaps multiple services in the church and multiple home groups within the church network. They remain "on location" so to speak.

11
Epilogue

This is a taste of some of my experiences in missions and the foreign mission field. The Lord prompted me to write about my journey, and I trust this information has brought you knowledge, encouragement, and confidence on your path of service for the Lord.

The Lord is who He says He is, and He will do what He says He will do. He is altogether trustworthy and if you hear His voice, you can rely on it. Seek God's confirmation and go in confidence. He is the Lord.

This is the beginning of your journey, and your experiences will add to the Book of Life.

Your Journey Begins now.

Go in Peace.